ON BEING A BISHOP

To, Derek

Roger Wilcke

'The saying is sure:
whoever aspires to the office of bishop desires a noble task.'

1 Timothy Chapter 3 Verse 1
NRSV

Roy Warke

On Being a Bishop

REMINISCENCES AND REFLECTIONS

the columba press

First published in 2004 by
the columba press
55A Spruce Avenue, Stillorgan Industrial Park,
Blackrock, Co Dublin

Cover by Bill Bolger
The cover image is a detail from the Clonmacnoise Crozier at the
National Museum of Ireland and is used by kind permission.
Origination by The Columba Press
Printed in Ireland by ColourBooks Ltd, Dublin

ISBN 1 85607 436 6

Table of Contents

Acknowledgements

I am grateful to many people who helped to jog my memory with accurate information. However they are in no sense responsible for the subsequent comments contained in the book.

In particular I would like to thank the Very Rev Michael Burrows, Dean of Cork, for his persistent prodding, without which the 'blissful idleness' of retirement as referred to by Archbishop McCann might have won the battle of intent.

My thanks also to my successor, the Rt Rev Paul Colton for his readiness to write a Foreword. I can only hope that his episcopal inheritance did not cause him too many sleepless nights.

As ever I am indebted to my wife, Eileen, for typing the manuscript and noting many a textual error. Some day I will master the art of thinking on to a computer!

Finally, my thanks to Seán O Boyle for his encouragement and insightful suggestions.

Foreword

Cork city centre, built on an island, embraced by populated hill-sides with their stepped laneways and steeples to the north and south, with the River Lee flowing from the west dividing to clinch the city centre on its island, and the harbour to the east, relies on its bridges. 'Cross the river' is a frequent direction to the lost visitor. More often than not that compounds the difficulty, for 'crossing the river' means two bridges (one onto the island and another off again) not one.

During his time in Cork, Bishop Roy Warke, like his neighbours in the Saint Fin Barre's Cathedral area (and indeed all Cork people) would have realised quickly that, navigating Cork is about, in part, knowing its many bridges: Cork's oldest (Clark's Bridge) being the closest to The Palace, then further downstream, South Gate, Nano Nagle, Parliament (built in 1806 to commemorate the Act of Union), Trinity, Parnell, Clontarf and Eamon deValera bridges, all on the south channel of the river.

Writing this foreword sits uncomfortably with the etiquette of never commenting on the work of one's predecessor. That I have been specifically liberated by the author himself to do so in order to introduce his latest work is both a responsibility and an honour. The key moment in this book comes, in my view, when the bishop, in Chapter 12 says "I reckon that my time in Cork was a period of bridge building ..."

As his successor, I can testify that this is so. In reaching this conclusion from the introspection of (an albeit energetic ministry within) retirement he displays immense self-awareness and perspicacity. The overriding sense in these pages is of a man, catapulted unexpectedly into the episcopacy, taking up residence in Cork's eighteenth-century Episcopal Palace, and from that home base having a far-reaching, embracing ministry internationally (through Lambeth and Christian Aid), nationally (in the Church of Ireland and Gaisce) and above all else, locally, in the work of the United Dioceses of Cork, Cloyne and Ross as well as in Cork city and county.

In broad terms, Bishop Warke's period in office was the 1990s: the time when much that was traditionally held in high regard, particularly in relation to the institutions and authorities of Irish society, came under deserved scrutiny and increasing suspicion. This era of consciousness of post-modernism was in itself a bridge time to some of the most rapid and radical changes humanity is discovering, not least in relation to itself.

As a bridge builder in a bridge time, Bishop Warke does much more in this volume than reminisce. He addresses the topics and events of his time with rigour. His remembering provides the springboard for prophetic challenge about Ireland, the church, Christian ministry and some highly topical issues: not least one which has an uncanny relevance in the context of current events within Anglicanism.

Since Bishop Warke's time I blessed one of Cork's newest bridges three hundred metres upstream from the oldest: it has been given the name St Fin Barre's Bridge; testimony to the fact that the Christian witness and succession to which Bishop Warke made his own faithful contribution in episcopal ministry, continues today.

I warmly and whole-heartedly commend this delightful book, and I know it will catalyse memories and nurture productive reflection in those who read it.

⳨ *Paul Cork*
November 2003

Introduction

The episcopal electoral college system in the Church of Ireland has much to commend it. Where once the focus was on the diocese, with the Diocesan Synod being the electing body, that focus has now been broadened to include representatives from the other dioceses in the province, and episcopal representatives from the two provinces. The necessity for a two-thirds majority of both lay and clerical representatives voting separately ensures that the person chosen has broad support within the diocese and the church at large.

The procedure is clearly laid out in the constitution, prefaced by a service of Holy Communion at which the presiding Archbishop, or a priest appointed by him, outlines the role of a bishop, and the guidance of the Holy Spirit is sought. The process is further undergirded by prayer on the preceding Sunday as parishes include the work of the college in their intercessions. Unlike the Church of England, the Church of Ireland allows for the possibility of the election of a woman to the office of bishop. This was enshrined in the 1990 Bill permitting the ordination of women to the priesthood, and given the calibre of those accepted for ordination it is only a matter of time before this possibility is realised, as has already happened in some other Anglican provinces.

Once the college is in session its deliberations are in camera, and in theory strict confidentiality is observed, unlike some other parts of the Anglican Communion such as America and Canada where the names of the candidates and the votes cast each time are open for all to see. Given the size and the family nature of the Church of Ireland, it is probably best that confidentiality is observed, although with the current stress on openness and accountability it may not be long before this procedure is challenged.

The first stage in the procedure is for the perceived needs of the vacant diocese to be outlined, and the type of ministry necessary to respond to those requirements. It must also be borne in mind that the person elected will be a bishop of the whole church and will be expected to make a contribution to the House of Bishops. Hence the value of a broad based electoral college.

After discussion of these matters, the president calls for names to be proposed. Those who so propose must be prepared to speak on behalf of their nominee.

Human nature being what it is it is inevitable that names will have been speculated on in the period prior to the meeting of the College, and it provides a fruitful field for conjecture, not least in the press. However, we have not yet reached the point where a certain American bishop is reputed to have hired a PR firm to promote his cause when a more prestigious diocese became vacant. Despite his efforts he was not elected, which could be interpreted as one up for the Holy Spirit! Irish politicking is probably more subtle, though possibly no less intense.

Once the merits of the candidates have been debated and their suitability analysed voting takes place. The procedure is determined by the president. Then, to quote the constitution Chapter 6 Part 1 Paragraph 13: 'If, on the taking of any vote, any person shall receive two-thirds of the votes of the members of each order present and voting, he shall thereupon be declared elected. If after the taking of several votes no person has received the requisite majority, the College may by a simple majority pass a resolution that no further vote be taken, and the appointment shall then pass to the House of Bishops.' It's of interest that two of the present (January 2003) House were appointed in this manner, the Bishops of Down and Dromore, and Clogher. If an election does take place the name is then passed to the House of Bishops for final approval.

Unlike some other provinces in the Anglican Communion, notably parts of Africa, episcopal elections in the Church of Ireland pass off with reasonable tranquility. The contrasting trauma of election in certain other provinces is obviously reflected in Resolution 51 of the 1988 Lambeth Conference under the heading 'Election and Retirement of Bishops and Archbishops.' Quoted in full it runs:

'This Conference:

1 Urges all Provinces to ensure that their provincial provisions for election and retirement of bishops and archbishops are unambiguous and are adhered to.

2 Recommends that, where problems arise regarding implementation of such provisions, and where such problems cannot be solved at the provincial level, the Regional Conferences of Primates should be called upon to advise, and if such conferences fail to solve the problem, the matter is referred to the meeting of the Primates of the Anglican Communion.'

Occasionally within the Church of Ireland there may be murmurs of surprise, one suspects even on the part of those elected. Certainly that was true on 23 November 1987, the date of the Cork electoral college. Having assured my wife that I would be home for tea I set out as one of the Dublin delegates for Christ Church Cathedral. Instead I found myself phoning her that afternoon with the news that we would shortly be taking the N7 to the deep south.

CHAPTER 1

Does God want Bishops?

At a training course for bishops back in 1990 the then Bishop of Salisbury, Dr Austin Baker, one of the leading theologians in the Anglican Communion, posed the question, 'Does God want bishops?' Given the composition of his audience it was a particularly provocative question. Fortunately for the reassurance of those present his ultimate answer was 'Yes'. But his 'yes' was predicated by a recognition that a bishop throughout his episcopate must be conscious of and reflect the declarations made at his consecration. These declarations place the emphasis on such matters as Holy Scripture, the doctrine of the Christian faith as the Church of Ireland has received it, the role of prayer and the various pastoral aspects of the bishop's life. But first and foremost and undergirding all else is the acknowledgment that God has called the person involved to this office. The question is very direct, 'Do you believe, so far as you know your own heart, that God has called you to the office and work of a bishop in his Church?' and the answer is a clear affirmation, 'I believe that God has called me.' It is this assurance of the call of God that helps to make life tolerable when at times the going gets tough.

At the 1998 Lambeth Conference each evening there was a video illustrating a particular aspect of a bishop working under stress. In some cases it had to do with a specific cultural or community setting as, for example, in Mozambique, with the related pressures of civil war. On other evenings it represented a more personal pressure as in the case of the Bishop of Rhode Island, Geralyn Wolf, who had to undergo a course of chemotherapy shortly after her consecration. As a follow on, at one of the small group sessions which were a feature of the conference, we were all asked to share some aspect of working under stress from our own situation. Among our diverse group of twelve we had a variety of experiences to relate, ranging from ministering to unemployed cod fishermen in Newfoundland to the Christian/ Muslim interface in Nigeria, with a tale of well-meaning but misguided missionaries in the Far East thrown in for good measure. But one bishop had only recently been appointed and said that he wasn't long enough in the job to have a story to tell. However he did volunteer some words of wisdom he had been given by a senior colleague on the occasion of his appointment: '85% of your time will be spent on mundane duties, for 10% of the time you will be on a high, 5% of the time you will experience the nearest thing to a living hell.' Give or take a few per centage points that is probably a reasonable summary of episcopal life, and it is at the times of the 5% one clings to the consecration affirmation: 'I believe that God has called me.'

Mention of the Lambeth Conference is a reminder that the Church of Ireland is an episcopal church. But what does this mean in today's world? So much depends on perception, and perception can be novel and even perplexing at times. Let me illustrate with a family incident.

One of the regular if not very profound features of each Lambeth Conference of Bishops is the taking of the group photograph. If it does nothing else it gives an indication every ten years of the growth of the Anglican Communion. It is also a visual indication of the shift of numerical power as the proportion of white faces continues to decrease. In 1998 we were dutifully instructed to appear in cassocks rather than choir robes as had been the custom previously. The resulting technicolour photograph hangs on the stairway of our home. Some months ago our grandson then three and a half was making his tortuous way down the stairs when his eye suddenly caught the photograph and he let out a cry of great delight, 'Oh! Look at all the Barneys.' For those who may be unfamiliar with Barney he is a much larger than life children's television character, amply proportioned and dressed in purple. For that three and a half year old the episcopal leaders of the Anglican Communion were a pack of Barneys – that was his perception.

In the public arena 'perception' has assumed a growing importance in recent years. For better or for worse 'image' has become vital in society: how goods are packaged; how candidates for a position present themselves. It's a trend given its ultimate expression by Alfred Heineken when he said, 'in the end life is all about advertising.'

This modern trend poses a problem for the church. How does it present itself with integrity to a secularised society without being completely sucked in to the whirlpool?

In a sense one casualty in this is the Lambeth Conference itself. Invariably there is a hectic rush to produce resolutions and therefore be perceived as doing something. This was certainly true in 1988 with seventy-three resolutions, including the one recommending the 'Decade of Evangelism'. While it was hoped, even anticipated, that the number of resolutions emanating from the 1998 conference would be reduced, such was not the case. In all one hundred and seven were compiled and the vast majority were voted on and passed. To a great extent Resolution 1.10 on human sexuality came to dominate both the Conference and post-Conference debate. As this is a subject which will not go away, but is likely to dominate both internal and external Anglican relationships for some time to come, the full text of the resolution is given:

This Conference:

(a) commends to the church the subsection report on human sexuality;

(b) in view of the teaching of scripture, upholds faithfulness in marriage between a man and a woman in lifelong union, and believes that abstinence is right for those who are not called to marriage;

(c) recognises that there are among us persons who experience themselves as having a homosexual orientation. Many of these are members of the church and are seeking the pastoral care, moral direction of the church, and God's transforming power for the living of their lives and the ordering of relationships. We commit ourselves to listen to the experience of homosexual persons and we wish to assure them that they are loved by God and that all baptised, believing and faithful persons, regardless of sexual orientation, are full members of the Body of Christ;

(d) while rejecting homosexual practice as incompatible with scripture, calls on all our people to minister pastorally and sensitively to all irrespective of sexual orientation and to condemn irrational fear of homosexuals, violence within marriage and any trivialisation and commercialisation of sex;

(e) cannot advise the legitimising or blessing of same sex unions nor ordaining those involved in same gender unions;

(f) requests the Primates and the ACC to establish a means of monitoring the work done on the subject of human sexuality in the Communion and to share statements and resources among us;

(g) notes the significance of the Kuala Lumpur Statement on Human Sexuality and the concerns expressed in resolutions IV.26,V.1,V.10,V.23 and V.35 on the authority of scripture in matters of marriage and sexuality and asks the Primates and the ACC to include them in their monitoring process.

The debate and the outcome, both in terms of the result (526 For and 70 Against) and the substance of the resolution, caused disquiet in the minds of a certain number of bishops. They were anxious to show concern for those affected by the outcome, and sought signatures for a letter to that end. It was proffered to a number of Irish bishops as we sat relaxing in one of the lounges of the Conference Campus, with the assurance (!) that it would have no real repercussions. Two things struck me at the time – the authors must have regarded us as very naïve, and this was a strange way for the Anglican Communion to do its business.

On the day following what was in fact a very fraught and intense debate on this resolution, we were requested to take up the issue of homosexuality in our small working groups. It was an interesting experience. For our four African colleagues it was a rather ostrich-like approach summed up by a phrase not unknown in the Irish context, 'what problem?' For them the issue did not arise.

The position of the two American bishops in the group was intriguing. One said that he would be right of centre. The other said that he had moved to left of centre. When asked why he moved he said it was because his diocesan financial adviser and treasurer, an admired friend of long standing with whom he had worked closely for years, had recently come out. And he made the point, the obvious point although not always fully appreciated, that when one puts a face, especially a familiar face, to an issue or problem, and cease to debate it merely in abstract terms, then it assumes a different perspective. It doesn't necessarily resolve the issue but it can alter one's approach to it.

Leaving aside the Lambeth context altogether, there is a very important concept enshrined in the point being made. Whether it has to do with overseas aid for developing countries or hospital beds here at home, once they cease to be debating points or political footballs and take on a human dimension, they assume a different priority and urgency.

We have been thinking of perception in a corporate sense as it relates to the Lambeth Conference and the resolutions that emanate from it, resolutions which have no legislative authority, only the moral strength derived from their source which is the ten yearly meeting of Anglican bishops.

There are, however, other facets of episcopal perception reflected, for example, by the House of Bishops and the work of individual bishops.

To take the work of the House of Bishops. Some years ago as one of our Church of Ireland press officers, in the days before a more professional approach was adopted, I anticipated receiving a communiqué from the secretary of the House of Bishops after each meeting of the House. At least that was the expectation. As it transpired the only communication ever received was a brief notification of the date of the annual Week of Prayer for Unity. At the time it seemed a very paltry return from such lengthy deliberations. It was only when I joined the House some twenty years later that I came to appreciate the reason for such a dearth of information. Much of the work of the House is of a highly sensitive nature, and demands a great degree of confidentiality if it is not to do damage to the lives of individuals. Furthermore, without this assured 'in camera' approach discussion would be inhibited, to the long-term detriment of the church.

However, the result of this is that at a time when the buzz words are 'transparency' and 'accountability' the House of Bishops is sometimes perceived as a type of club, carrying on its business behind closed doors. One sensed that this perception was heightened in 1990 when the bishops exercised their constitutional prerogative and voted as a separate House on the Bill permitting the ordination of women to the priesthood, and further exercised that prerogative in simply announcing their approval without indicating the result of the voting.

This rather introverted perception of the House of Bishops is one with which the members will have to live despite the modern clamour for openness. Certainly members of the church have a right to expect a little more than the annual notification of the Week of Prayer for Unity, but to expect total transparency would to some extent undermine the nature of the Church of Ireland as an episcopal body.

This undermining of the episcopal role is evident in other areas of church life also. It is particularly so in relation to liturgical practice where, if constant comments are anything to go by, there is frequent departure from the institution undertaking to use the prescribed orders of service of the Church of Ireland. Certainly there is flexibility allowed in the more modern forms of service, but liturgical flexibility is not to be equated with rampant individualism where all sense of liturgical balance is discarded. So often it is the liturgical order of the Church of Ireland that attracts those searching for a vehicle of spirituality. Undoubtedly this was true of St Fin Barre's Cathedral, Cork. It seems strange that forms of service which have been painstakingly produced by the Liturgical Advisory Committee can be nonchalantly mutilated.

Another area where the episcopal role is diminished relates to the remarriage of divorced people in church. Legislation is now so framed that the opinion of the bishop must be sought by the rector involved based on the facts of the particular case. However the rector is under no obligation to accept the bishop's opinion. While it is helpful for a rector of have an authoritative reference point if he or she wishes to deny the request of a couple, it could be a cause of tension if bishop and rector are not of the same mind. Indeed there might well be some who would take a delight in acting contrary to the wish of their bishop.

One of the roles that a bishop values most is that of *pastor pastorum*, and given the comparatively small numbers of clergy in each diocese, even in the larger ones, this is very much a characteristic of clerical life in the Church of Ireland. Clergy who come from outside Ireland, sometimes from dioceses with up to six hundred clergy, have commented favourably on the availability of the bishop in their new sphere of work.

In recent years the question of clerical stress has been highlighted, and to cope with this new situation diocesan mediation panels have been set up along the lines of the 'three just men' in the medical profession. At the time of my retirement in 1998 this was still in embryonic form and so I had no direct experience of its implementation. However, I did express some reservations that it could undermine the relationship between bishop and clergy, by inserting a structure, albeit an expert structure. No longer would the bishop be the first port of call in a time of crisis. It is, of course, true that a bishop is not necessarily an expert in stress management, but I would reckon that every bishop has access to someone who is, and in approaching the problem in this way the *'pastor pastorum'* relationship is in no way diminished, indeed may well be enhanced.

In cases where the relationship between bishop and cleric does break down it is necessary that there be some formal mediation process available. If this was on an *ad hoc* basis it would mean that recognition could be taken of the particular circumstances of the case and the mediator/s selected accordingly.

One other area where the church, through its General Synod, unwittingly undermined the episcopal role was in the Bill setting up the Commission on Church Buildings, but this will be dealt with in Chapter 8.

It is of interest that fifty years ago the theological argument exercising the minds of church people related to the question of whether episcopacy was of the *'esse'* or *'bene esse'* of the church. Such specifics no longer surface with the same cogency. Nonetheless we must be careful lest the episcopal role is so undermined that the Church of Ireland loses one of the distinctive features of its identity.

There is one element of episcopal collegiality which may not be fully appreciated except by those directly involved, and that is the mutual support within the House of Bishops. Whereas the role of a bishop as *pastor pastorum* is often stressed, the question of who pastors the Father in God is not always considered. It is within the fellowship or collegiality of the House that this pastoring can take place and often does. This is necessary because of the nature of a bishop's work. It is essentially a lonely office.

The consequence of the consecration service is to some degree reflected in words from John Betjeman's poem 'On the Investiture of the Prince of Wales':

You knelt a boy and rose a man
And so your lonely life began.

Two factors tend to heighten the experience of episcopal loneliness. The first is the fact that in the Church of Ireland we have not gone down the road of appointing assistant bishops within the diocesan structure, even though this has been occasionally suggested, especially in relation to the two Archbishops. While recognising that numerically this makes sense, it does mean that the local bishop can be isolated, even though he can turn to archdeacons and deans for support and sodality.

The second factor is the perception that many people have of a bishop as a managing director who can hire and fire. This springs, I believe, from the prelatical perception associated with the Roman Catholic hierarchy which has come to be identified with Church of Ireland bishops also.

On more than one occasion it was said to me, 'Bishop, it wouldn't happen in business', when the ministry of a parochial clergyman was being called into question by parishioners.

However, a bishop is not a free agent who can act in an arbitrary fashion on all matters. He is limited on two fronts. At his consecration he solemnly promises all due reverence and canonical obedience to the Archbishop of the province and his successors. He is also bound by the canons and constitution of the Church of Ireland, which in fact place a rector in a very strong and secure position once he or she has been instituted to a parish. It follows that one of the most important episcopal roles is that of chairing boards of patronage when rectors are nominated to vacant parishes. An unsuitable appointment can have long-term adverse effects on the life of a parish. I well recall one occasion when we were having difficulty filling a rural parish and the prospects were not hopeful. As I discussed the situation with the parochial nominators one of them commented with commendable pastoral wisdom, 'better an empty house than a bad tenant.'

In any discussion of episcopal isolation and loneliness it is important to remember the family involved and in particular the spouse. This was highlighted for me at Lambeth 1998 by the plight of Sylvestre Tibafa Mugera, Bishop of Kisangani in the Congo, who was a member of our working group of twelve. He was a small, very reserved man who could speak very little English and depended on one of the group from Kenya to keep him in touch with what was being said. During the conference the civil war in the Congo escalated to such an extent that the bishops from that part of Africa were unable to return home directly. They were domiciled in Nairobi for some weeks. When news of the escalating war reached Sylvestre he tried to get through to his family in Kisangani by phone but was unable to do so. His concern for their lives was palpable. As we tried to offer what support we could through the fellowship of our group and our wives, my mind kept going back to something the Archbishop of Canterbury, Dr George Carey, said about bishops' families: 'Our ministries can be so absurdly demanding that they can take us away from our families, and this can have the tragic effect of taking them away from God.'

A bishop as *pastor pastorum* has a primary concern for his clergy and their families, and rightly so. But as with a rector in a parish, so with a bishop in a diocese, he must be alert to the strains imposed on his own closest relationships. It can happen that what is developing before our eyes is veiled from our sight.

Because of the ever-increasing demands made upon the episcopate, the words of George Carey are of distinct relevance.

These demands are reflected in the expertise now required to fulfil roles which in times past were often regarded as little more than token appointments, for example as chairmen of school and hospital boards, not to mention the time consuming nature of the work. In such cases it is essential to have experienced personnel in positions of responsibility, who can deal with the complexities of modern legislation.

A further demanding sphere is that of ecumenism, both at home and abroad. At home the visible relationship between church leaders is vital in giving a lead, while the requirements of international representation are increasing both in terms of inter-Anglican commissions and networks, and talks on a broader ecumenical basis. While it may not always be necessary to have episcopal representation, there are occasions when such participation underlines the importance attached to the work involved.

The Church of Ireland has played a significant role at the international level in recent years through its episcopal representatives on such bodies as the Eames Commission, the International Anglican Liturgical Consultation and the Central Committee of the World Council of Churches. At the enthronement of Dr Rowan Williams as Archbishop of Canterbury the blessing of the new incumbent of Augustine's seat was given by Archbishop Eames as the senior Primate of the Anglican Communion. In addition Bishop Colton (Cork), before his consecration, was the Church of Ireland representative at the Porvoo conversations with the Baltic Lutheran churches. In the same context it would be remiss not to mention the role played by the late Archbishop McAdoo as Joint Chairman of the first Anglican Roman Catholic International Commission (ARCIC).

It falls to the lot of bishops to receive much correspondence. In the midst of what is sometimes hypercritical and occasionally vitriolic, there can appear a more positive communication. Such was the case recently when I received a letter from a monk in England. He has lived outside Ireland for about sixteen years and admits to being a little out of touch, but he goes on, 'It does strike me, however, that there is a growing spiritual vacuum in Irish society and that the Church of Ireland is perhaps well placed to provide for the spiritual needs of many. With its Christocentric emphasis, moderation and integrity, it is ready to play a greater role in Irish society.'

This is indeed a daunting challenge, especially for a church which, at least in the South of Ireland, has probably not more than 3% of the population, and that within a fairly narrow sociological compass. However, even more challenging than both these factors is the current apathy displayed towards institutional religion and reflected in the fall in church attendances. Not that this apathy is confined to Ireland. At Lambeth 1998 the Bishop of Colorado, based in Denver, one of the winter playgrounds of the USA, summarised it as akin to 'playing squash against a haystack'. A picturesque but potent analogy, and one with which many a cleric in Ireland could identify. However, it is unlikely that this apathy will be banished unless the church is perceived to be relevant, and the church is only relevant to the world in so far as it is different from the world and challenging worldly assumptions, otherwise it will go on playing ecclesiastical squash against the secular haystack.

One aspect of Church of Ireland life that has always fascinated me is the frequent sniping at bishops from within the ranks of our own church, which is usually coupled with the accusation of being 'out of touch'. Yet from whence do the bishops come? Invariably they come from the ranks of the parochial clergy, and bring with them a wealth of experience at the coalface of church life. In fact I know of no other province in the Anglican Communion where this applies to the same extent. Indeed, occasionally it is used as a basis for criticism by those who view episcopacy in more academic terms. This is not to say that there is a lack of intellectual strength on the Bench. Far from it, not least at the present time. Rather it is to stress the depth of parochial experience available which suggests that those who cry 'out of touch' are perhaps a little out of touch themselves.

At the end of the day, people's episcopal perception is less likely to focus on the Lambeth Conference and the House of Bishops and more likely to focus on individual bishops, and how they measure up in the public arena. That is the nature of society today. Given this it is interesting to reflect on some words written by that doyen of broadcasters, Alistair Cooke, about Adlai Stevenson. Stevenson had twice stood as a United States presidential candidate in a country where losers receive little kudos. On both occasions he was defeated. Despite this Cooke could write of him, 'What he left behind was something more splendid in a public man than a record of power. It was simply an impression – of goodness. He had mastered the art, far more difficult and rarer than that of a successful politician, writer, musician, actor; success as a human being.' Does God want bishops? If he does, one suspects that he wants them to be truly human.

CHAPTER 2

Pulpit Politics

In an article in the *Church of Ireland Gazette* (7 January 2003) that redoubtable columnist 'Cromlyn' pointed to the danger of a division within the Church of Ireland along north/south lines, based not on political affiliation but on liturgical practice.

Those of us who have ministered in both jurisdictions, and also have ancestral roots both north and south, are very conscious that this unseen divide is no new phenomenon. It may have manifested itself in different ways at different times but it has always been there. I well recall on coming south in the mid-1950s having served a curacy in the north, being told by a contemporary northern colleague that the clergy in the south didn't really know the meaning of work! Year after year at the General Synod, despite the camaraderie of the diverse members, there is a very discernible distinction between those who come from the north and the south, not least in their reactions to liturgical and political issues. In general this has become more pronounced over the last thirty years as the terrible events in the north have impinged on the lives of both clergy and laity, a situation sadly aggravated by the fact that any comment from the south appears to be viewed by some as criticism from a position of ignorance.

This divide was also evident in the work of the Church of Ireland Youth Council. For ten years as President of the Council I was conscious of this more in terms of an undercurrent rather than an overt factor, but one felt sad that even in the relationships between the younger members of the Church of Ireland there should be signs of this unseen divide. However, it is only fair to say that the divide usually centred around the allocation of administrative posts and places on committees, and in this their attitude simply reflected that of many of their elders.

Let me go back in time. For a number of years in the

parochial ministry in Dublin I made a point of inviting a northern cleric to preach whenever possible, on special occasions,
until one day a leading parishioner, whose opinion I valued, re-
marked that he was getting tired of political lectures from the
pulpit. What in fact was happening was that those who came
down from the north felt they had to allude to the political situation there for the enlightenment of the southern congregation;
indeed the very fact that they had been invited probably gave
that impression. But there was a tacit assumption that people
living south of the border could not appreciate or understand
what was happening in the north, and as a corollary were not in
a position to make an observation. I was sometimes reminded of
a comment made as far back as 1960 to a group of students in
New York by the then Archbishop of Capetown, Joost de Blank.
It was at the height of the apartheid campaign, and to those who
were reluctant to condemn or even comment from a distance his
advice was along the lines that they had an obligation to do so.
His point being that where basic human rights were being in-
fringed the Christian above all others has a duty to raise the
issue. 'Never feel that because you are removed from the situation therefore you cannot comment on it.'

What the scenario on this island did reflect was a quasi-polit-
ical division within the Church of Ireland. But together with this
there developed a hypersensitivity to honest and sincere comment from fellow churchpeople in the south. While it was inevitable that such comment would vary in stridency, for the
most part there was a genuine wish to understand and come to
grips with what was happening in the north. This was reflected,
for example, in the decision of the Diocesan Council of Cork,
Cloyne and Ross in May 1997 to link with the diocese of Clogher
rather than with a diocese outside Ireland, as was common practice. It was felt that while this might not be as attractive in ecclesiastical jet setting terms, it was what was required to help inform
the diocese of the complexities of life in the north. Clogher was
viewed as appropriate as it was a diocese with a mix of urban
and rural parishes not unlike Cork. While recognising the value
of linking with a diocese such as Clogher, it was also important
from a Church of Ireland point of view not to become introverted.
This was reflected in the resolution on Companion Dioceses

(2.3) passed at the 1998 Lambeth Conference, which runs as follows:

This Conference:

(a) notes that many dioceses in the Anglican Communion
have not as yet been able to establish companion relationships;

(b) believes that the time has come for significant new initiatives in encouraging all dioceses to develop companion relationships across provincial boundaries, as part of the process
of developing the cross-cultural nature of the communion;

(c) believes that, in addition to the structures administered
through Partners in World Mission and the Anglican
Communion Office, dioceses should be encouraged to take
initiatives in sharing information, contact and exchange;

(d) accordingly resolves that each diocese of the Communion
should, by the time of the next Lambeth Conference, have
made a serious effort to identify one or more dioceses as a
companion, in formal and informal ways.

One further delicate factor in the equation at the time of the
Clogher link was the concern among Church of Ireland people
in the south that the perceived intransigence which manifested
itself each year at Drumcree would be ascribed to them also, and
the good community and inter-church relations which had been
painstakingly built up over the years would be undermined or
at least damaged. This was something which may not have been
fully appreciated by those in the north. It is one thing to proclaim and take pride in the unity of the Church of Ireland as an
All-Ireland institution when events run smoothly, but when tur-
moil appears in one area care must be taken that the hoped for
short-term gulf does not become unbridgeable. Nor should it,
given, for example the two-way movement of clergy between
north and south. At one point in the mid-1990s in Cork diocese
50% of the clergy had served part of their ministry in the north,
while of the current House of Bishops eight out of the twelve
have parochial experience of serving in both jurisdictions. This
clerical mobility should provide a reservoir of insight to help
with mutual understanding, and so forestall not just the development of an ecclesiastical fissure within the Church of Ireland,
but also disharmony within the community.

Arising out of recent events there has developed what might be described as a genre of political preaching. In his General Synod presidential address of 1991 the Primate challenged the Church of Ireland to ask a very direct question of all its activities: 'Is it relevant?' The response to this has tended to foster political comment, both from parochial pulpits and episcopal rostrums. There appears to be a belief that unless a sermon or address has direct political reference it is not relevant. In all this there is a danger that the underlying Christian elements are sidelined, and the church is seen as just another player, and a minor one at that, in a complex political game. Even worse, it is possible that the pulpit may be used to feed the prejudices of blinkered individuals. It was at the 1988 Lambeth Conference the then Archbishop of Canterbury, Dr Robert Runcie, said that one purpose of the church was to bring a gospel critique to bear on society. In other words it was the duty and task of the church to ask the hard questions based on the principles that conform to the mind of Christ as revealed in scripture, and in particular the four accounts of the gospel.

There will be occasions when specific issues will have to be addressed, and not to do so would deservedly render the church irrelevant. But there is a danger in this, a danger which was summarised succinctly by Bishop Jerry Winterrowd of Colorado at the 1998 Lambeth Conference. The setting was a sectional meeting where small working groups came together under the chairmanship of Rowan Williams and attempted to give input and structure to the sectional report under the heading 'Called to live and proclaim the good news.' The meetings tended to be chaotic and dominated by vocal bishops with issues to air. In the midst of this babble of conflicting voices with their diverse issues Bishop Winterrowd, at the close of one session, stood up and quietly commented. 'You cannot build a church on issues; you must build a church on the gospel.' This is a thought expressed more recently by the Bishop of Tuam, Dr Richard Henderson in the Anglican Cycle of Prayer – 'Pray for modern evangelists, who will lovingly and intelligently apply eternal truth to today's human beings in truly contemporary situations.'

Yet how tempting it is to be drawn into issues and allow them to dominate church life and even absorb the ministry of a bishop. Society, and the media in particular, are very happy to focus in on issues, and the more sensational the better. These issues can be both internal and external. The former may relate to such matters as church plant, liturgical practice or clerical peccadilloes, and the latter to political or community affairs. Not that these issues and many others are unimportant. Far from it. But it must not be a case of addressing issues for the sake of addressing them. It must be done relative to basic Christian principles, or to put it in another way, there is a need to theologise before commenting. Without that the trumpet will give an uncertain sound, and the church of whatever tradition is unlikely to hear repeated the words of Zechariah (Chapter 8 Verse 23): 'Let us go with you for we have heard that God is with you.'

CHAPTER 3

Ireland's Opportunity

The old political slogan 'England's difficulty is Ireland's opportunity' has taken an interesting ecclesiastical twist in recent years with the influx of a growing number of English clergy, both male and female, to the Church of Ireland.

There has always been a certain number, not least in the West Cork area, where an apparent wish to escape from the reputedly more impersonal type of ministry in our sister church is often coupled with a search for an ecclesiastical Shangri-la. It's a search pursued by a variety of practitioners as the appearance of a diversity of meditative centres testifies.

This influx of non-native clergy has been hastened by the contract type of ministry in parts of the Church of England which appears to leave those involved out on a limb at the end of their contract period. Having such clergy in the Church of Ireland has both negative and positive aspects.

On the negative side there is the disadvantage of not being a cradle member of the Church of Ireland, and therefore not having an empathy with its ethos, which admittedly is indefinable, even by those who most frequently use the term. It has been said that the ethos of the Church of Ireland resembles the subtlety of a lady's perfume in that one is not really conscious of it when it is present, but it is missed when absent. The matter is further aggravated by the fact that this ethos has in large measure been conditioned by a negative reaction to the practices of the Roman Catholic Church at disestablishment. One of the fascinating features of church life today is that while the Roman Catholic Church appears to be tending towards simplicity in, for example, matters of dress and liturgical practice, the Church of Ireland is becoming more ornate. Because of this lack of home produced clergy it is all too easy to cause offence and alienate parishioners. Not that this is peculiar to non-nationals, but they are undoubtedly at greater risk.

Furthermore, from the point of view of those making appointments it is more difficult to obtain an accurate picture of those applying from beyond these shores. While in most cases there is no problem, there have been examples of ecclesiastical square pegs in the parochial round holes. The difficulty is that once a person has been appointed within the Church of Ireland it is well nigh impossible to take corrective action, a fact not always appreciated by parishioners or the wider community. It is worth noting the actual position as outlined in Chapter 4, paragraph 31 of The Constitution of the Church of Ireland.

A clergyman duly admitted to a cure shall be deemed incumbent thereof, and shall not be removable except in accordance with

(a) a resolution of the diocesan synod, approved by the bishop, that there is no longer sufficient work in the cure to justify its continued existence as a separate benefice, or

(b) a decision of the Court of the General Synod, or

(c) the provisions of section 36 of this Chapter (i.e. on reaching the age of retirement)

With regard to paragraph (a) The Constitution states than an incumbent shall not be removed until he has been offered a cure which is not less suitable.

However, no matter how conspicuous the negative aspects may be, they are far outweighed by the positive.

Up to fairly recent times the Church of Ireland has been a comparatively monolithic structure in terms of its ministry. While a small number have undergone their theological training outside the Church of Ireland the vast majority were trained in the one institution, the Divinity School of Dublin University, and more recently the Church of Ireland Theological College. This meant that there was a reasonable uniformity of ministry. This was coupled with a strictly limited liturgical range of expression which existed until the Liturgical Advisory Committee began its work in 1962. While this combination had the merit of continuity and uniformity it also had within it the peril of monotony at a time when minds were opening up to new ideas and travel was providing people with opportunities for fresh and innovative liturgical experiences.

Into this local setting have come a number of clergy from beyond these shores, and their varied experiences have helped the Church of Ireland meet the challenges posed by modern developments. In a sense what is happening in society is being mirrored in the church, and just as society in general is grappling with pluralism so too the church is having to come to terms with a pluralist ministry, sometimes failing to appreciate that whatever threats this may hold, real or imagined, are far outweighed by the refreshing insights brought by those who help us to see ourselves as others see us. It's sometimes forgotten that it is not so long ago since it was a virtual impossibility for clergy to cross diocesan boundaries, let alone penetrate the ministry of the Church of Ireland from outside. Yet how much poorer we would be, not just numerically but also episcopally, without this leavening of the ministerial lump. Proportionally speaking there cannot be many contemporary provincial benches of bishops that could rival the Church of Ireland in terms of variety of ministerial experience both nationally and internationally.

CHAPTER 4

Baggage Handlers

On the morning of our departure from the 1988 Lambeth Conference buses ferried delegates from the campus of the University of Kent to the railway station at Canterbury. As my wife and I watched the delegates and spouses getting into the buses one American bishop appeared with what was the biggest suitcase I have ever seen. This was his baggage.

It's a scene I often reflected on during my time as a bishop. We all bring baggage with us: political, cultural, theological, liturgical, spiritual. Over the years I have seen baggage being totally divisive at parish level, as a new broom seeks to sweep clean the perceived archaic practices of the past.

Often a new rector is aided and abetted in this by the institution sermon, frequently preached by a like-minded individual, without any acknowledgement of the ministry that has gone before. It was a former Bishop of Connor, the Rt Rev Arthur Butler, who exercised his prerogative and preached at all institutions in his diocese. One suspects that he did this in order to emphasise the sense of continuity in parish life, and to remind the incoming rector that he or she would be building on what had gone before.

In reflecting on these matters my mind goes back to my early ministry and before. While training for the ministry in the Divinity School of Dublin University there were two organisations which canvassed members: the Evangelical Union (EU) and the Student Christian Movement (SCM). Early on I took a conscious decision not to join either, and so preserved a freedom of theological and liturgical expression. I have never regretted that decision, certainly not in more recent times where there appears to be a growing emphasis on party labels with a consequent weight of baggage leading to polarity at parochial and even diocesan level.

Early on in my ministry in a North of Ireland parish I had occasion to preach in a neighbouring parish where the rector, originally from the south, was one of the most senior and highly respected in the diocese. As we talked over a cup of tea he proffered some advice based on his own experience, and it was, not to join any of the orders which were strong in the area. It was important, he maintained, to preserve one's autonomy, and whatever the future might hold by way of preferment to ensure that one was not behoven to any particular group. It was another way of saying don't become encumbered with any political or cultural baggage. To do so would inhibit comment and criticism. While recognising that the church is the whole people of God, it is still true that for many the clergy represent the voice of the church, and the authenticity of that voice is diminished if it is identified with any one group or organisation.

What is true of clergy in general is certainly true of bishops in particular. Whatever baggage may be brought to the position it must be carefully and sensitively applied. Within a diocese there is invariably a wide range of traditions and opinions reflected both in the composition of clergy and parishes. While bishops cannot be expected to jettison their baggage completely, thereby risking the diocese becoming an amorphous conglomeration with no real focus or direction, neither must they so impose their personal predilections that people feel dragooned in ways that undermine the faith and practice which may have sustained them over the years.

One way in which this is sometimes expressed is 'you can only lead from the centre'. What this means in effect is that a bishop more than most has to perform a diocesan balancing act. It may be inhibiting to natural instincts, but that may be the price that has to be paid.

While we all bring baggage with us there can be occasions when the baggage we accumulate *en route* comes to dominate our ministry in an obsessive manner. Some examples of this were evident at Lambeth 1998. For me two examples stood out. The first was the Bishop of Lahore, Alexander Malik. Each time I heard him speak he returned to the same theme: the problems for a Christian minority in a predominantly Muslim State. It almost seemed that his accumulated baggage was too weighty to carry. However, subsequent events have borne out the reality of his concern, as Christians have been murdered as they worshipped in church.

The second example was the Primus of Scotland, Richard Holloway, for whom the issue of human sexuality had assumed dominant proportions. Allowing that it is a subject as divisive for the church as Iraq is for the international community, for Bishop Holloway it represented baggage that seemed to accompany him wherever he went.

CHAPTER 5

Naughty Clergy

A phrase, coined I believe in the Church of England, to describe clergy who have stepped out of line (usually in the sexual context) is 'naughty clergy'. Of course it is not just in sexual matters that clergy can be naughty as some well-publicised events in the Church of Ireland indicate. However, whatever interpretation is placed on the word 'naughty' it invariably reverts to the bishop to resolve the issue in question.

This raises the whole question of episcopal oversight or the bishop in his/her traditional role as *pastor pastorum*.

In this we must go right back to the very beginning, to the initial choice of candidates for interview prior to training. Although the selection process has altered in recent years there is still a grave onus on those at the parochial and diocesan levels to be absolutely rigorous with potential candidates. This is never easy given the pastoral relationship between, on the one hand, the rector and parishioners, and, on the other hand, between bishop and clergy, especially in the smaller dioceses. There can be a temptation to let those at the next stage of examination take the hard decision.

However, while the hard decision is more likely to be taken at the national level, it is not always so. This may reflect a genuine hope and even belief that the candidate will develop and mature during training. 'After all,' it is said, 'isn't the time of training a time of testing also?' But testing by whom? No doubt there are some who have turned back having put their hand to the plough of theological training, but personally I am only aware of two such cases.

As an aside it might be added that there is no more difficult episcopal duty than having to inform a candidate that he/she has not been recommended for training. Unless one is directly involved in the selection process it is impossible to know the full facts, and without these not only is the bishop placed in an awkward position in informing the candidate, but the whole process can be called in question by those with restricted theological agendas to pursue. Having been involved with the selection process on a number of occasions, both as bishop and parochial cleric, I have no hesitation in attesting to the absolute fairness with which the process is conducted, an opinion backed up by a senior personnel officer in a large industrial plant, who himself was a candidate for ordination. Assuming that a candidate is recommended and begins training – what then?

Fifty years ago the vast majority of those entering the ministry were single young men who came straight from secondary school, took a degree at Trinity College, and emerged from the Divinity School with a Divinity Testimonium. The exception (and some were notable) was the mature student, and the absolute exception was the married student. Today the mature married student is more likely to be the norm. The growth in late vocations has been a feature for some years now. In order to enter the theological college they may have given up well paid secular positions, and for many it entails a sacrificial way of life not just for themselves but their families.

But in the context of training as a time of testing it poses a major problem. What if they or the staff, and in particular the staff, conclude that they should not continue? Boats have been burned, but nonetheless the church has a responsibility having permitted the person to start on the road of training. What we have in fact done over the years is create the impression (even illusion) that training must automatically lead to ordination. In the vast majority of cases this is what happens, but it needs to be clearly spelled out to those who have passed the hurdle of selection that this does not inevitably lead to ordination. Without this clear understanding situations can arise which are not just embarrassing, but in the long run may not be in the best interests of the church.

What is called for is a rigorous continuous assessment, not just academically, but related to all those elements which are so much a part of parochial life in the Church of Ireland such as liturgical, pastoral, recognition of authority, personal relationships, capacity to work.

One recognises that these are difficult aspects to assess, but it is at this point that the principle of assessment or oversight must be inculcated; otherwise ordinands emerge without any sense of their responsibilities in the ministerial framework. This is exacerbated by the contemporary practice of just one curacy and then appointment to a parish. No longer is there the luxury of a post-ordination training period as provided in the field, so to speak, by two or three rectors. No matter how well structured post-ordination training courses may be, there is no substitute for time spent in a parish with an experienced colleague. Even the valuable and varied experience brought by mature students requires to be honed to the needs of parochial life.

The principle of assessment is one which does not rest easily on clerical shoulders. There is an inbred independence which has developed over the generations, and any attempt, for example, by the bishop to exercise *episcopé* or oversight is viewed with suspicion as a type of big brother intrusion.

Yet in so many other professional arenas assessment has become a regular feature, not least in the teaching profession, with which the ministry is often compared in terms of stipend.

It was during a training course for bishops in England early on in my own episcopate that I discovered a method of review, which if adopted could serve a useful purpose in the Church of Ireland. It was based on a preliminary questionnaire which sought to ascertain those aspects of ministry with which a rector was most comfortable, and those which he found most difficult, together with any perceived needs with which it was felt the bishop or the diocesan authorities could help.

Armed with the replies to the questionnaire the bishop then visited the rector. First the ministry in that parish was affirmed, and by concentrating on comfort areas the rector felt more confident and at ease. This led on to areas of difficulty, not in a judgemental sense, but simply with a view to helping the rector cope by sharing concerns. It's inevitable that individual rectors find some aspects of ministry more congenial than others, and the main purpose of the episcopal visit was to assist in those areas where there was self-confessed need. Sometimes rectors are reluctant to come to their bishop with a problem. Perhaps they are afraid that it will be viewed as a sign of weakness. Whatever the reason the longer a problem remains unresolved the more likely it is to cause really serious trouble. At least this approach can help to pre-empt that situation.

A further result is that once rapport has been established there is the possibility that latent concerns may emerge, concerns which in the isolation of ministry can develop a cancerous like quality.

The difficulty in all this is that a bishop exercises a dual role, that of *pastor pastorum* and that of overseer, and occasionally the two roles clash. But even then, if there has been a proper understanding of the relationship between rector and bishop, there should not be complete alienation. So much depends on the right understanding being instilled from the point of initial training onwards.

Having said all this it might well be asked, 'But who assesses the bishop?' In one sense it could be argued that in any diocese there are as many assessors as there are clergy, not to mention critical laity. However, in terms of accountability there is none, other than the constitution, within whose framework the bishop exercises oversight. In pastoral terms there is the House of Bishops, within whose fellowship individual bishops can be supported in times of stress. In recent years one has sometimes heard strident criticism of the collegiality of the House of Bishops, but allowing for the autonomy of each bishop, the fraternity of the House is one of its most supportive assets.

CHAPTER 6

Strength in Depth

It is common practice nowadays for football managers to speak of strength in depth as a necessity for success. It is a concept with which I can empathise as during my time in Cork we had a clerical team whose combined strengths were exceptional, and provided singular resources within the diocese. In addition to expertise in such areas as the bible, liturgy, spirituality, mission, communications and inter-Anglican relations, one cleric had made an in-depth study of the New Age movement which was widespread in parts of west Cork. Add to all this the fact that four members of the diocesan clergy were appointed to the House of Bishops and one begins to realise the depth of talent available within the diocesan family, a fact which often added zest to discussion at the annual clergy conferences at Myross Wood Retreat centre. A further barometer of excellence was that three members of the diocese served on the Anglican Consultative Council, thereby bringing a refreshing breadth of vision to our deliberations. One of the three was a layman, Canon J. L. B. Deane, whose contribution to the life of the Church of Ireland has been immense. For twenty five years he acted as a lay secretary of the Standing Committee, and in that capacity he towered over the General Synod, ensuring that the affairs of the chief legislative body of the Church of Ireland were conducted with rigorous correctness. It was a matter of enormous comfort to have him as assessor at the Diocesan Synod for eleven years.

If there was strength in depth among the clergy, the same could also be said of the laity. Whether it was finance, property, legal affairs, education or any of the myriad facets of diocesan life, Cork could call on some of the leading practitioners in these areas. This was to be seen not only at the more high-powered level of the Diocesan Council, but also in the membership of the profusion of ancillary committees which go to make up the life of a diocese. In common with the Church of Ireland in general, time and expertise were given willingly, something which betokened a great affection for the diocese. Shortly after my appointment as bishop I received a letter from a leading member of the laity in Cork who indicated that I was coming to the best run diocese in the Church of Ireland, and my best policy was to let it continue in that vein. At the time I wasn't sure whether to interpret it as a dire warning or good advice. Over the years I came to the latter conclusion, as it became apparent that administratively the diocese stands very high, due in no small measure to the efficiency of the Diocesan Secretary, Mr Wilfred Baker. While it is true that in so many areas the bishop bears ultimate responsibility, one could always be sure that the factual basis and presentation of those decisions, however unpalatable, were such that no mistrust could ever be levelled.

In two other areas the strength in depth of the diocese was also evident, and this was at the General Synod and Diocesan Synod.

Each year the General Synod marks a high point in the life of the church for those involved. I say 'for those involved' advisedly, as since retirement I am not sure how great an impact it makes on the 'person in the pew'. So much depends on what is reported in the press. There was a time when one could depend on an extensive report of each day's proceedings, but latterly, apart from the Primate's presidential address, and the traditional 'off-guard' photo of one or both of the archbishops, there has been a paucity of reporting. It has to be sensational or politically pungent before it merits inclusion in the papers. This probably reflects the surfeit of religious news in recent years, which contrasts dramatically with the media scene thirty or forty years ago.

But what of Cork in relation to the General Synod?

Those elected to represent the diocese do so conscientiously and regularly. Despite having to travel long distances a percentage attendance in the nineties is maintained year after year. At a time when revision of membership is contemplated it is vital to scrutinise attendance figures. There is not much point in increasing representation unless the percentage attendance can also be relied upon.

But not only did Cork delegates attend, they also contributed hugely in debate, and there were times when but for the Cork contribution deliberations would have been very dull indeed. These informed contributions were in no small measure due to the traditional pre-synod briefing meeting attended by the delegates.

If the high point of church life is the meeting of the General Synod, the ultimate high point for those in the deep south was the holding of the General Synod in Cork in 1994. The request to do so followed from the holding of the Synod in Belfast for the second time. With true Cork self-belief it was felt that the Lee was not going to be outdone by the Lagan.

There was some apprehension both within and without the diocese, mostly without. Would delegates travel the distance to Cork? It had to be pointed out that it is the same distance from Cork to Belfast as it is from Belfast to Cork, and the Cork delegation had travelled north in force. As it turned out it was one of the best attended Synods on record, with many people from all over Ireland making a week of it. On the Sunday before Synod as many bishops as were available preached in the diocese, and the opening service in St Fin Barre's Cathedral was a model of its type, owing much to the then Dean, Dr Richard Clarke. The City Fathers also played their part and the Lord Mayor, John Murray, hosted a reception in the City Hall, while the purpose built conference centre at the Silversprings Hotel proved to be a wise venue: near enough to the city to be convenient, but far enough out to deter any would-be shoppers from slipping out!

By way of preparation for the Synod the Communications Committee visited Cork, and Ted Crosbie generously hosted a lunch at the offices of *The Examiner*. The name Crosbie has long been associated with Cork's newspaper which in recent years has changed its name twice in rapid succession from *The Cork Examiner* to *The Examiner*, and then *The Irish Examiner*. In general relationships with the press were good, even if at times the mildest critical comment was portrayed as 'Bishop slams'.

By tradition the most junior bishop conducts prayers at the General Synod each morning, and for six years I had this duty to perform. It was an indication that for a lengthy period there was a settled House of Bishops. What a change there has been in recent years, and since 1999 six new bishops have been appointed; a turnover of 50%.

At one particular Synod I used prayers from 'Bread of Tomorrow', a book of prayers edited by Janet Morley of Christian Aid relating to the world's poor. The prayers made a marked impact on many members, so much so that orders for the book outstripped the supply available on the Christian Aid stand. Since then a number of clergy have commented on how valuable a resource the book is.

As indicated earlier, a focal point of the Synod is the opening address by the President, the Archbishop of Armagh. It provides an opportunity to engage with whatever issues may be exercising the mind of the church at that time, and to give a lead in dealing with them. The variety and complexity of these issues is reflected to some extent by the lengthening of the President's address since he took up office in 1986. It is also indicative of the globalisation of Anglican structures in recent years, and the need to keep the church at provincial level in touch with developments worldwide. Forty years ago presidential addresses were much more parochial in character, and apart from reference to the Lambeth Conference there was unlikely to be any great emphasis on international events.

If the strength in depth of the diocese was emphasised by delegates to the General Synod, the same was also true of the Diocesan Synod. Attendance by both lay and clerical members was invariably excellent with never more than a handful of people missing. Business at Diocesan Synods is of necessity fairly mundane, but even the dullest report can be enlivened by oratorical excellence, and such was invariably the case. As happens at the General Synod current events were often addressed by means of motions and resolutions and this was particularly true of the political situation in the north of Ireland, about which there was a very genuine concern, particularly in relation to the role of the Church of Ireland.

By means of the presidential address one sought both to reflect on the past year and also spotlight current topics. Although not peculiar to Cork, one area of constant concern was the condition of the farming community. Basically Cork is a rural diocese and farming is at the heart of its life, highlighted by the fact that the Minister for Agriculture comes from West Cork. At the end of the day it would be my hope that anyone researching the place of the Church of Ireland in Cork would find relevant material in the eleven presidential addresses delivered between 1988 and 1998.

The Diocesan Council is in many ways an extension of the Diocesan Synod, and at its four meetings throughout the year the ongoing business of the diocese was transacted. I was informed early on that one of my predecessors, Gordon Perdue, went on the theory that as people had come from a distance to attend he wanted to given them full value. As a result meetings which began at 7.00 p.m. rarely ended before 11.00 p.m. Happily I inherited a revised version, and there was a rule of thumb that 9.30 p.m. was the cut off point, and we usually managed to adhere to this timetable. One way of doing this was to preclude AOB.

Much depended on preparation, and in this I was fortunate in being well briefed by the Diocesan Secretary, Wilfred Baker.

The one point that I was always anxious to stress was that those elected to the council by Synod were not parochial representatives with a local agenda. However difficult it might be to divorce oneself from local church politics it was essential for the Council to be seen to be acting in the best interests of the diocese. I was particularly conscious of this as some parishes were unrepresented while others had a number of members.

I well recall being asked by a member of the press immediately after my election what my hopes were for the diocese. I had hardly recovered from the shock of the vote, and I replied that my hope would be for a happy diocese. More and more I came to realise that this depended to a great extent on the integrity of the Diocesan Council whose decisions affected the life of every parish. I was blessed by the calibre of the members and nowhere was strength in depth more vitally illustrated than in the make up of the Diocesan Council.

CHAPTER 7

Close Encounters

Even allowing for civic pride there are few buildings of greater beauty on this island than St Fin Barre's Cathedral, a fact affirmed by John Betjeman who described it as 'a gem', and attested to by the large number of photographers who delight in its outline, especially as seen from The Palace avenue. This beauty together with the high musical standard maintained by the choir, under the direction of Colin Nicholls, ensures that the injunction of the psalmist is truly fulfilled: 'Worship the Lord in the beauty of holiness.' (Psalm 96 Verse 9)

The present building is the third to stand on the historic site associated with the foundation of the city by St Fin Barre in the seventh century. Although the cathedral of the minority, it is closely identified with the city and when in 1998, during a period of restoration, the famous Golden Angel was stolen there was general consternation. Happily it was quickly found and eventually restored to its prominent position, ready, as local tradition would have it, to give warning of the end of the world half an hour before the event, thus ensuring that Corkonians would have a head start on the rest of humanity!

The present cathedral owes much to Bishop John Gregg who performed the dedication ceremony in 1870. It was a remarkable act of faith given the circumstances of the time. The effects of the Great Famine must still have been felt. The Church of Ireland was coming to terms with disestablishment and morale was at a low ebb. Yet despite all this John Gregg pressed on with this building project designed by William Burges. By all accounts Gregg was a remarkable man both as a preacher and motivator, and the cathedral stands as a monument to his tenacity. He was later succeeded by his son, Samuel, and the name Gregg is perpetuated in the area by the designation of one of the nearby

roads, Gregg Road. Indeed the whole area has something of a
Close atmosphere with the dean and organist living in Dean
Street alongside the cathedral, and the bishop living across the
road in The Palace dating from 1782.

It was this juxta position of bishop's house and cathedral that
did much to enhance one's time in Cork. The city was within
walking distance and enabled one to feel a part of the community
in a way that would have been impossible if the residence had
been located in one of the more distant suburbs. I always felt
that this was a factor not fully appreciated by the central church
authorities who made various attempts to dispose of the house.
Bishop John Buckley often spoke of his envy of the fact that I
could walk the streets of Cork and not have to rely on the car.

Having said all that, it did highlight the almost Gilbertian situation whereby the bishop's house is the responsibility of the
central church body but the diocesan authorities have a virtual
veto over any suggested change. It is easier to be dogmatic if one
does not have financial responsibility! It was during my time in
Cork that a new system was devised. An annual allocation was
made from central funds and a local committee was charged
with the task of using it to the best advantage. My wife and I
were fortunate in the calibre of the Cork committee and the system worked well. We were also fortunate in having as a moni-
tor, Mr Denis King, who acted on behalf of the Representative
Church Body, and whose professional advice was invaluable in
detecting and anticipating problems before they assumed un-
wieldy proportions. There are not too many people who would
relish being phoned at 7.30 on Christmas morning to announce a
burst water main, the result of a ferocious storm on Christmas
Eve 1997 which had also removed part of the roof of the cathedral.

The scourge of old buildings is dry rot and there was a major
outbreak in 1989. It necessitated radical repair to a large section
of the house. Happily, as we thought, the work coincided with a
three week trip we were making to the United States to celebrate
our silver wedding anniversary, and we were assured that the
work would have reached a liveable stage on our return. The
day after our departure a stop was put on the work, and we returned to a scene resembling a building site. Such was our home

for the next number of months before common sense prevailed and the work recommenced. Fortunately there were just two people living in the house, but it did mean that for a lengthy period visitors were *verboten* and relationships with 'the powers that be' reached a nadir.

However, such episodes sometimes serve to enhance the ultimate pleasure of the surroundings. Set on a hill the view over Cork city is magnificent and the house itself, despite its size and age, had a homely atmosphere. The two public rooms, dining room and drawing room, were a real bonus, and between them could absorb up to one hundred guests.

Among those guests on a regular basis were the Lords Mayor and visiting Ambassadors. Cork has the privilege of having a Lord Mayor as distinct from a Mayor and has been well served over the years. During my time just one woman held the position of first citizen and that was Chrissie Aherne, who brought a distinctive homeliness to the office.

The annual visit afforded an opportunity to exchange views on a variety of topics, and coming at the start of the Lord Mayor's term of office invariably laid the foundation for a good working relationship throughout the year. For example, it was as a result of the visit of Frank Nash that the diocese initiated the link with the diocese of Swansea and Brecon as a complement to the city's twinning with Swansea. In addition each Lord Mayor willingly received any ecclesiastical VIPs who happened to be in the diocese as was the case when the Primates of the Anglican Communion met in Ireland and those from New Zealand, Uganda and Japan spent a weekend in Cork. It's of interest to recall that the Primate of Japan was scheduled for Cork as Archdeacon Michael Mayes, now Bishop of Limerick, had spent eight years in Japan and could speak the language; another example of the strength in depth of the diocese.

The ambassadorial visits often brought a sense of drama as the special branch 'cased the joint'. This was particularly true on one occasion when the British Ambassador, Sir Nicholas Fenn, was due to call. It was at a time when the situation in Northern Ireland was especially tense. My wife went out to remove some washing from the clothesline only to find herself confronted by soldiers in the bushes. On reflection the grounds of The Palace were readymade for anyone with evil intent, but happily the visit passed off without incident. Incidentally, Sir Nicholas was a devout Anglican and insisted on visiting St Fin Barre's Cathedral before leaving the area. Just a few years later at the installation of Dr Michael Jackson as Dean, the cathedral welcomed Dr Rowan Williams as preacher. Two of our good friends who stayed with the preacher at The Palace now take great delight in informing their friends that they 'breakfasted with the Archbishop of Canterbury'.

The cathedral hosted many memorable services including ordinations, one of which was that of the Rev Janet Catterall, the first woman priest to be ordained in the Republic. Another notable occasion was my enthronement service in 1988. It was not without its lighter side when the great West door stuck as I knocked for entry. The occasion was also a reminder that we were very much strangers in a strange land, as my wife was asked for her invitation as she entered the cathedral! It wasn't until some weeks later that she arrived home one day from shopping in the city happy in the knowledge that for the first she had been greeted in her own right. Such are the non-theological factors of episcopal existence.

Observance of the church's liturgical year is one of the characteristics of the Anglican way of life, giving a balanced presentation of the faith. The observance was very obvious in the life of St Fin Barre's. I particularly looked forward to the Easter services commencing with the Easter vigil on Holy Saturday. The dramatic movement from darkness to light was a vivid reminder of the great triumph to be celebrated on the following day. And what better way to celebrate the resurrection that by singing the Hallelujah chorus from *The Messiah*. In the setting of the Easter Eucharist that chorus took on real and moving significance. It was not a performance as can so often be the case, but a great outpouring of joyful thanksgiving in the setting of the church's highest act of worship.

I always felt that there was little need for a sermon after the singing of the Hallelujah chorus, but by tradition a bishop preaches in his cathedral on Easter Day. My final Easter morning was to prove interesting. The Good Friday agreement on Northern Ireland had been signed two days before, and there was a renewed sense of hope abroad that peace would at last be secured on this island. I had been approached by the press for a comment. 'Did I think the agreement would work?' I replied by saying, 'Come back to me in five years time and I will be better able to answer that question.' I mentioned this incident in the course of my sermon on Sunday only to be verbally assailed after the service and accused of displaying pessimism at a time of great optimism. I have often thought of that scene outside St Fin Barre's during the subsequent five years, and especially as the political parties in the north and the representatives of the British and Irish governments attempt to find agreement about the agreement. Whether it is a question of not wanting to recognise the divide or a lack of real engagement, there is, I believe, a great failure on the part of many people in the south of Ireland to understand the depth of division in the north. To the political pragmatist in the south used to compromise, it is illogical. But to most northerners on both sides of the divide compromise is simply viewed as weakness; yet without it can there be a solution? The words of Archbishop McCann back in the 1960s have an ominous ring of truth about them. Asked when he thought the northern problem would be solved, he replied, 'Never in a thousand years.'

There is always a danger that a cathedral, especially one as beautiful as St Fin Barre's, will be viewed simply as a tourist attraction, when in fact it is a sanctuary of the living God whose worship is carried on day by day and week by week. Of necessity my travels throughout the diocese took me away most Sunday mornings, but Evensong in the cathedral was something to be anticipated with relish. It is one of my fondest memories of Cork, and to be able to relax in the context of ordered worship was indeed a privilege.

However, it must not be forgotten that there were three cathedrals in the united diocese, and each one had its own distinctive features. St Colman's in Cloyne was of massive proportions and, given the rural nature of its setting, it is difficult to imagine the totality of the building being used for worship. At present it is only the choir stalls that are used.

Dating from the twelfth and thirteenth centuries it was once said that 'the secluded quiet of Cloyne is refreshed by memories of saints and scholars.' Foremost among these was of course George Berkeley, Ireland's greatest philosopher, who was bishop from 1735-52, although one surmises that the memory of Christy Ring of hurling fame is more deep-rooted among the locals of today.

It's reported that when George Simms was appointed Bishop of Cork, Cloyne and Ross in 1952, Professor A. A. Luce, an authority on Berkeley, wrote congratulating him on being appointed to Cloyne!

The ancient cathedral came into its own each year at the Christmas candlelit carol service. The nature and size of the building lent an atmosphere that was almost surreal.

As with so many of the ancient buildings which the Church of Ireland has inherited great credit was due to the dean, the Very Rev George Hilliard, the select vestry and parishioners for their fortitude in addressing the problems of maintenance.

However, try as they might they were never able to obtain permission to dispose of some of the excess communion silver in their possession, which would have eased the financial burden. At times the opening words of the Priorities Report of 1979 came back to haunt us: 'The first priority of the Church of Ireland is spiritual not material.' Yet when we seek to utilise some of our surplus material possessions in a practical way to sustain the worship of the church in a rural area, we are met with strong opposition from within.

One of the finest views in West Cork is to be had as one approaches Rosscarbery from Clonakilty, a view somewhat diminished by the construction of a modern hotel at the far side of the distinctive causeway. As one rounds a corner in the road the village comes into view in the hollow, and nestling there with its spire reaching heavenwards in dramatic symbolism is St Fachtna's Cathedral, described by Bishops Day and Patton in that literary gem *The Cathedrals of the Church of Ireland* as 'a comely building containing some ancient features'. They go on to conclude that 'there is a charm about this minor cathedral church, so remote from the busier centres of life'.

As with many West Cork churches St Fachtna's benefits from summer visitors, but it also has a sizeable all year round congregation characterised by a surprisingly large number of children.

By cathedral standards it is comparatively small, and this lends itself to a homely atmosphere, despite the fact that a bishop's daughter was murdered there in 1643! Like St Colman's, a highlight of the year is the candlelit carol service at Christmas, which for many from the surrounding parishes is a traditional meeting point.

There is a close-like atmosphere in the setting, with the deanery and parochial hall being adjacent to the cathedral. During the tenure of Dean Richard Henderson, now Bishop of Tuam, a library was set up which further enhanced the cathedral as the mother church of the diocese.

A feature common to all three cathedrals was the happy relations with the Roman Catholic clergy in each area. Major cathedral services were coming to be viewed, not in exclusive terms, but almost as community events.

Perhaps the most outstanding of these was the annual St Patrick's Day service in St Fin Barre's followed by a reception at The Palace. The service, which dated from Bishop Perdue's time, was attended by the Lord Mayor and Corporation in full ceremonial robes, together with representatives of all aspects of city life. Latterly it took the form of a eucharist, and it was a sign of the times that the vast majority of those attending communicated.

I always felt that the day should have been an occasion for an ecumenical liturgical gesture, and I know that some who spoke to me felt the same. However, because it is a Roman Catholic holy day of obligation there had to be Mass in the North Cathedral. This meant that after a somewhat rushed reception the official entourage crossed the river to another service. I'm sure that in time this anomalous situation will be amended, and the good ecumenical relations that exist will be given more visible patronal expression.

CHAPTER 8

Church Closures

Some years ago, in 1967 to be precise, St Nicholas's church, Dunlavin, celebrated its 150th anniversary. As rector of the parish at the time and to mark the occasion I produced a small booklet outlining the history of the church and parish. Included was the following comment: 'When the history of the Church of Ireland in the twentieth century comes to be written it may well be that parochial re-organisation will figure prominently in its pages.' Little did I appreciate how relevant those words were to be in relation to my own future ministry.

On moving from Dunlavin in 1967 to the Dublin northside parish of Drumcrondra and North Strand with St Barnabas, just after the closure of St Barnabas's church, one soon became aware of the deep attachment the people of the East Wall area had to their parish church. However, at the same time these was a realism present, typical of the people of the area, and to their credit they became fully integrated into the life and worship of their new spiritual home, the Ivy Church as it is affectionately known by the locals. This realism was also exhibited when St Barnabas's church was eventually demolished having suffered vandalism, as it stood unused in a very vulnerable location.

Later as Archdeacon of Dublin I had the task of chairing the Parochial Reorganisation Committee which sought to come to terms with the changing needs of the diocese. As we met with a great variety of parochial representatives and sought to plan for the future, it was very clear that most people wanted to retain the *status quo*, and many a rearguard action was fought. Looking back and witnessing the changes that subsequently took place, sometimes through force of circumstances, one realises the number of ministerial working hours that might have been saved and more profitably used.

On being elected Bishop of Cork, Cloyne and Ross in 1987 I

was left in no doubt that the diocese was over churched and action would have to be taken. Arising from this, one of the first
events to be encountered was the visit of the Commission on
Church Buildings. This body had been set up by General Synod
in 1986 and given absolute powers once it was invited into a diocese. It consisted of representatives from every diocese in
Ireland under the chairmanship of the then Bishop of Cashel
and Ossory, the Rt Rev Noel Willoughby.

The idea for such a commission had originated in Cork,
where in the mid-1970s there had been a radical reorganisation
of parochial boundaries and a planned reduction in clergy, without any corresponding attention to church buildings. When the
Commission was proposed in General Synod I don't recall any
members voting against it. The Cork representatives could
hardy do so, and those from the other dioceses probably
thought it would never affect them. The Bill was viewed as un-
contentious and went through 'on the nod'. Certainly I was one
of those who voted in favour, little realising the pivotal role it
was to play in the years that lay ahead. Having spawned the
idea there was an obligation on Cork to invite the Commission
into the diocese. This the Diocesan Council did at its meeting on
9 July 1988. Because of the absolute powers vested in the
Commission, and because responsibility for the implementation
of the final report rested with the bishop, I asked what would be
the case if the bishop disagreed with some elements of the report. The reply of the Council was that I was obliged to act. Even
at that early stage it was obvious there could be problems, as
there are few more difficult tasks than having to champion a
cause to which one does not fully subscribe. I well recall dis-
cussing this possibility with a senior bishop at the time, and his
comment was to the effect that he didn't think he would find it
convenient to implement the report of the Commission until
after he had retired!

The principle of church closures is one which people can
readily accept in general terms; it is when one comes down to
specifics that problems arise. And so it proved to be when the
final report was issued in 1989. As drawn up by the General
Synod Bill, the Commission had a positive brief which was to
determine the number of churches required for the worship,

work and witness of the Church of Ireland in a diocese. However, it was inevitable that this would be interpreted by many in negative terms of church closures. Twenty churches were in fact scheduled for closure, with a small number given a reprieve for three years, before a final decision was made.

In general this depended on the state of repair and upkeep of the listed churches and much work was done in the intervening period with positive results. Probably the most outstanding example is to be seen in Blarney where closure was threatened. To leave the Church of Ireland without a visible witness in one of the country's major tourist locations seemed to me to be the height of folly. Under the leadership of the then rector, Harold Miller (now Bishop of Down and Dromore), a complete renovation and refurbishment of the church was carried out. Today with its adaptable ambience it stands as a monument to vision, enthusiasm and commitment, and its multipurpose possibilities are fully utilised by parish and community. Twenty churches were in fact closed, including sixteen of those originally scheduled.

It appeared that the criteria of the Commission were largely statistical, and in some cases at least a more thorough investigation of the local situation would have saved much subsequent heart searching. For example, the title of ownership was not absolutely clear in certain cases and in such situations to close a church with no immediate prospect of sale would leave the building open to vandalism. However, in not closing all the churches the bishop was left vulnerable to misunderstanding and the accusation of favouritism or a bowing to pressure.

What are some of the lessons that can be learnt from this painful episode?

(1) In general it is better if change can have its genesis locally. While it is true that the idea of a commission emerged at a diocesan level the real impact was felt at the parochial level, and despite the protestations of the Commission there was a feeling that consultation was minimal, and the local voice was not being heard. To express it in colloquial terms the consultation had the appearance of a flit visit. It's not without significance that the Commission has not been invited to act in any other diocese since the initial invitations from Meath and Kildare and Cork.

(2) The closure of a church is traumatic and an occasion of sadness for the parishioners involved, some of whom may have roots in the building going back for generations. In preparing them for the event the role of the rector was vital, and in Cork there were some examples of a wonderful reconciling ministry, so that when the day for closure arrived there was a genuine sense of thanksgiving for the past and a determination to face the changed circumstances of the future.

(3) Closure brings out the best and the worst in those involved. For some, not necessarily those with deepest roots in the area, it can become a crusade in which a variety of ploys ranging from emotional blackmail to orchestrated campaigns are used to put pressure on the bishop, together with the recurring threat of 'going to the media'.

(4) Over and over again in relation to the Church of Ireland one hears of our attachment to buildings, and few would deny this. It is generally spoken of in derogatory terms, when in fact there may well be an attachment that signifies something deeper than the superficial observer would understand. The difficulty is to recognise and be sensitive to those whose sense of loss is genuine. The negative side is reflected in a comment made by a rector, 'All they want is for me to open the church on Sunday. It wouldn't matter if I just did half a dozen handstands as long as the church was opened.'

(5) Over twenty years ago a leading layman of the Church of Ireland estimated that at least fifteen million pounds was spent each year on church maintenance. The sum today would be much greater. Given this enormous figure it behoves the Church of Ireland to look long and hard at requirements in terms of plant. The days of needing a church every two miles or so to facilitate those whose means of transport was limited to the pony and trap and 'Shank's mare' are long gone.

(6) One of the most oft quoted comments when closure is mooted is that it will be seen as 'letting the side down' in relation to the majority Church, although one senses that this has less validity today than in former years when, for example, Cork city was ringed with massive new church buildings by Bishop Lucey. However, the plus side is that with fewer churches worship can become a much more vibrant and corporate occasion,

not to mention the removal of pressure from many a cleric or lay reader who has to spend Sunday morning in a mad dash from service to service with little or no opportunity to meet parishioners, let alone maintain a good standard of worship. Indeed, as pointed out by the current Bishop of Cork, Bishop Paul Colton, the new emphasis on speed limits and penalty points places many rural clergy at risk.

(7) It has been said that the Irish countryside is littered with the ruins of churches that have been closed, and this is very true. It appears that in the past roofs were removed and the buildings left to disintegrate, but due to the solid nature of the structures many are still standing and in some cases are a real eyesore. There are in fact three options. The building can be sold for an appropriate use, it can be retained and used by the parish, or it can be demolished. In Cork all three options were utilised, although once a building is sold its future use is unpredictable, especially if it is sold on to a third party whose idea of an appropriate use may differ radically from that of the church authorities

One of the uses most often canvassed is that of a library, but as the late Archbishop McAdoo once said, 'There is a limit to the number of libraries a city can maintain,' and it is a cause of sadness for many to see the uses to which some churches have been put. While demolition at first sight might not be an attractive option it may well be the lesser of two evils.

(8) The way the Bill inaugurating the Commission was drawn up placed the bishop of the diocese involved in an invidious position. On the one hand, he had no option because of the terms of the Commission, which were absolute. In a real sense his authority within the diocese was eroded, a fact not always appreciated or even acknowledged by the people of the diocese, and certainly not understood by those outside the Church of Ireland. In retrospect it seems strange that this was not questioned by the members of the House of Bishops in 1986 when the Bill was proposed. On the other hand the responsibility for implementing the final report rested with the bishop at a time he deemed convenient. The intention may well have been to help the bishop by giving him some flexibility, but all it did was confuse the issue by giving the appearance of choice when in fact no real choice existed. The only choice was to procrastinate, and

this was contrary to the intention of the Bill, even though as already indicated, the reasons for not acting in certain cases were valid and authentic. The Church of Ireland places great store on its episcopal character. It is not an exaggeration to say that in this respect the Commission acting *in loco episcopé*, usurped the role of the bishop, and thereby diluted the influence which the bishop had in his own diocese. Certainly it created a situation which was time absorbing and deflected attention from areas of work which I have no doubt would have been more spiritually profitable to the diocese. It was ironic that the diocese should have been absorbed with the issue of church closures at the very time when the Anglican Communion as a whole was responding to the Decade of Evangelism, which sought to move people's thoughts and actions from maintenance to mission, from retrenchment to outreach.

There is no doubt that this whole experience left parts of the diocese with a feeling of dejection and isolation, rather like Elijah of old under the juniper tree. One way to counteract this was to help people see, in a tangible way, that they were part of the larger whole, and that the diocese was not moribund. To this end, and with the expert backing of Charles Harris, who was the Church Army representative in the diocese, a great rally was organised at the Green Glens Arena, Millstreet, where the Eurovision song contest had been held. Permission was given for all churches to close on the chosen Sunday and every parish was requested to mount an exhibition. Because of a change of date at very short notice, the Primate, Archbishop Eames, was unable to be with us as had been originally intended. However, due to the biblical principle of importunity on the part of Charles Harris, the Primus of Scotland, Richard Holloway, took his place. At the time he was engaged in one of his occasional jousts with the media and this added colour to the visit. His sermon based on ' The Prodigal Son' was much appreciated by upwards of 4000 members of the diocese who had gathered for the occasion.

No matter how serious the situation, there is always a lighter side, and this is reflected in two incidents. The first occurred during an intense debate on the Commission's Report at diocesan synod. One of the contributors was a farmer from West Cork

who produced an analogy from the soil as he counselled cau-
tion, 'Bishop, always remember that when thinning turnips you
have to be careful not to pull up the strong ones with the weak.'

The second was a letter from a very irate parishioner whose
church had been closed. It contained a threat to set up a rival institution within the parish. The letter then concluded with the
time-honoured ascription. 'I remain your obedient servant!'

CHAPTER 9

All work and no play

West Cork is renowned as a holiday area, and to facilitate the seasonal influx of visitors a number of churches opened during the summer months including Crookhaven, Baltimore, Glandore and Courtmacsherry. Each had its own distinctive charm and traditions. St Brendan's Church, Crookhaven, had developed the tradition of an evening epilogue during July and August. It was a delightful setting with the sea forming a natural backdrop through the plain east window, and one suspected that some who might not be regular worshippers found a renewed sense of the presence of God on their visit to the Mizen.

The harbour at Baltimore plays host during the summer to boats from many places and one particular Sunday sticks in my mind. The church bell rang out across the harbour, and just as the service began some people in sailing attire joined the congregation. It transpired that they were from a French yacht that had arrived the night before. They heard the bell on board, and came to land to join in the worship. Their action was a real challenge to many a landlubber.

The church of St John the Evangelist, Courtmacsherry, welcomes a number of regular visitors each summer, and like the other churches in the diocese it is conscientiously cared for by the local congregation. However, one of my most vivid memories of Courtmac was of a hazardous journey from there to Clonakilty one very wet Sunday morning. I was advised of the quickest route over the hills, but as the rain poured down not only were the roads flooded, but the water coming down from the hills began to uproot the surface before our eyes. Eventually, after attempting a couple of alternative routes, we arrived in Clonakilty well behind schedule, to all round relief.

I well recall my first visit to Christ Church, Glandore. It was during one of those prolonged spells of good weather that occasionally grace an Irish summer. The setting on that Sunday morning was idyllic as one looked out from the small churchyard down the sun-drenched bay. So impressed was I that my wife and I returned the following day to savour the experience again.

The one church outside the confines of Co Cork was St Paul's, Ardmore, and it too catered for a summer congregation. During my time the village had the distinction of winning the Tidy Towns' Competition, and the local congregation played their part in having the church and churchyard well up to standard.

Two other summer experiences were memorable. One was the annual open-air service on Cape Clear Island. It is not always possible to hold the service in the open, but when it is the atmosphere is truly unique. It is on Clear Island that Chuck Kruger, an American teacher, has settled having found his utopia off the coast of West Cork, from whence his writings and contributions to Sunday Miscellany have enriched the lives of many.

The other experience centres on St Barrahane's Church, Castletownshend, where there is an annual summer musical festival. The church is set on a hill and one must climb fifty-two steps to reach it. However, it is well worth the climb and provides a delightful setting for the festival which over the years has hosted some of the leading musicians both nationally and internationally, including Peter Sweeney, who was so impressed by the organ he played one Sunday morning while on holiday that he returned to give a recital.

With so many holiday delights available close at hand, the temptation was to think less about one's own holidays. However, one holiday proved to be memorable. It was a trip to the Holy Land led by the then Bishop of Meath and Kildare and later Archbishop of Dublin, Dr Walton Empey.

For some time my wife and I had harboured a wish to visit the Holy Land, but were reluctant to do so in case our image of the holy sites would be shattered. From childhood a certain picture of the biblical lands had been created and nurtured.

At last we took the plunge and signed up for the trip. We

were helped by a friend in Christian Aid who reminded us that two thousand years had passed since the time of Our Lord and to temper our expectations accordingly.

Our visit coincided with the signing of a peace accord between Israel and Jordan which created a sense of euphoria, and meant that we could cross from Israel to Jordan with the minimum amount of red tape. President Clinton visited Jerusalem for the signing, and our group felt a part of the occasion as our coach driver was seconded for the day to drive the American party.

Of the many highlights three stand out from a biblical perspective. The first was the drive from the airport at Tel Aviv to Jerusalem. As we rounded a bend in the road Jerusalem came into view for the first time, set on a hill, and the words of the psalmist took on fresh significance: 'I will lift up mine eyes unto the hills.' Although many years have passed since the pilgrims of Old Testament times ascended to Jerusalem the vision has retained something of its original intensity. At least that was so for one modern pilgrim.

The second highlight centred on a visit to Mount Nebo in Jordan from whence Moses viewed the promised land of Canaan. As one stood and gazed across the Jordan valley to Jericho, the city of the palms, one was conscious that geographically little had changed in all those years. The scene created a deep sense of awe, and in purely historical terms was the highlight of the trip as the centuries simply rolled back.

The third highlight occurred when we travelled north to the Sea of Galilee or the Lake of Tiberius. As was traditional Holy Communion was celebrated by the lake. As we worshipped there in that biblical setting, around a curve in the shoreline a boat appeared with two men casting their nets into the sea. At that moment time stood still and we were transported back two thousand years. Again it created a deep sense of wonderment and reverence.

As we visited the traditional sites associated with the life of Our Lord we were grateful for the advice of our friend in Christian Aid. There is an undoubted tourist atmosphere, as is inevitable, and one has to make a conscious effort to recapture the spirit of two thousand years ago. On the other hand much has not changed as the three highlights listed indicate. It is this combination of the ancient and the modern that adds authenticity to the total scene. If all was changed utterly it would be impossible to recapture the tone of yesteryear, but if nothing had changed there would surely be an aura of unreality. One of the misfortunes of the current situation in the Middle East is that the cradle of Christianity is no longer available for the safe nurture of modern pilgrims.

CHAPTER 10

'You always have the poor with you'

Within the House of Bishops, portfolios are allocated by the Primate. As a result one of my tasks was to chair the Bishops' Appeal Committee for almost eleven years, and a most satisfying task it was.

The Appeal dates from 1972 and was set up as a means of responding to the needs of the Third World both in terms of relief and development. From comparatively modest beginnings (£22,000 was raised in 1972) it has grown on a reasonably regular basis, and in 2002 over €900,000 was donated by members of the Church of Ireland. In a real sense, the response to the Appeal acts as a barometer of the church as a caring community.

Ireland has always stood high in world rankings regarding response to emergency appeals, and the fact that there was a fund available meant that the Church of Ireland could make an immediate response in times of crisis. But the Appeal Committee were always anxious to stress the value of development projects, and much thought was given to the allocation of funds in order that a balance would be maintained between relief and development. From 1978 a block grant arrangement was initiated with Christian Aid and each year 50% of grants were channelled through that inter-church agency which works in conjunction with local partners in sixty countries worldwide. In this way there was accountability for the grants made.

All grants are submitted to the House of Bishops for final approval before being paid, and it is of interest that in 1984 the arrangement with Christian Aid was reviewed by the bishops and the wish expressed that all monies should be available for discretionary distribution. However, it is still very much the 'rule of thumb' by which the committee works, and indeed Christian Aid may have benefited from the review. It certainly has not suffered.

One of the dilemmas in reporting to the bishops was the difficulty of conveying the depth of debate in arriving at the allocations. But at least there was a regular episcopal presence on the committee which had not always been so, and this acted as a two-way conduit of comment.

With the increase in income and the growth in grant applications, it was decided in 1991 to divide the role of secretary between administration and project analysis. This latter role was filled by Canon Desmond Harman who over the years had amassed an immense fund of knowledge and background information, as well as a capacity to sift the truly meritorious from the less justifiable. In this he was often aided and abetted by Elizabeth Ferrer, a very remarkable woman whose insight into such matters was invaluable, and whose stature in this field could be gauged by the fact that for a number of years she presided over CONGOOD, the umbrella body for non-governmental organisations (NGOs) in the South of Ireland. But not only was Elizabeth a much valued member of the committee, her home was also a haven for many an overseas visitor and student in times of need. For many people the test 'I was a stranger and ye took me in' (Matthew Chapter 25 Verse 35) took on real meaning when they came in contact with Elizabeth Ferrer.

Looking back over the history of the Bishops' Appeal, the committee has endeavoured to respond to the various challenges presented to it. It has provided a means whereby the Church of Ireland as a whole can exercise its caring obligations; it has sought to promote the cause of world development through a system of diocesan representatives appointed by individual bishops; it has endeavoured to educate the church at large both by means of appropriate literature and the appointment of an education agent; it has provided additional methods of tax efficient giving whereby people can contribute; it has updated its methods of presenting its reports by the use of pictorial images; it has responded to increasing administrative demands due to increased income by the appointment of a part-time treasurer; it has sought to co-operate with other agencies and in that way exercise political pressure.

While taking all this on board, the committee was conscious that it had to keep on asking honest and searching questions both of itself and of the church at large. What, for example, are the expectations of the church? Occasionally one was conscious that the Bishops' Appeal Committee was being viewed primarily as a collecting agency in times of emergency, or simply as a means of making a quick response so that the Church of Ireland could be seen to be doing something.

Is long-term development given adequate space in the church's thinking when immediate response to crises is much more media friendly? Does the Bishops' Appeal fire the imagination of people, especially young people, or is it diminished because it is not a 'hands on' organisation? It does not have workers in the field and so the emotional appeal is reduced because the involvement is always second-hand.

As a result is there a case for spending more on publicity, especially as there is competition among the agencies? Indeed it is a question that might well be asked, are there too many agencies or NGOs? One cannot help but conjecture at the multiple administrative costs as one listens to the various appeals made from time to time in response to such events as famines and earthquakes. But good quality publicity is costly and it has always been the policy of the Bishops' Appeal Committee to keep such costs to a minimum. So much depends, not just on the work of diocesan representatives, but also on the wholehearted support of the parochial clergy.

In general the policy of the committee was that it did not allocate funds to individuals. However, this placed the Primate in an embarrassing position as occasionally he received requests of this nature, especially from his fellow Primates. The sums were not necessarily large but there was a principle involved. As a result, the Bishops' Appeal Committee recommended that a Primate's Contingency Fund be initiated which would enable him to respond immediately to individual requests as he saw fit. This was set up 1994 and is now a routine item in the Representative Church Body report.

One of the recurring debating points since the inauguration of the Appeal in 1972 has been its title. While many have expressed dissatisfaction, pointing out that it can be misleading, no one has yet come up with a viable alternative. It's of interest that the members of the Advisory Committee set up back in the

early 1970s to make recommendations regarding an Appeal
were conscious that it needed an 'imaginative title'. Such ideas
as Church of Ireland Concern (CIC) and Celtic Aid were floated,
but their report records that the committee was not in a position
to make a unanimous recommendation on this point.

Earlier it was pointed out that in 1978 a block grant arrangement was initiated with Christian Aid. This was a reminder that
the Church of Ireland's association with Christian Aid goes back
many years.

Christian Aid began its life as a response to the needs of
refugees in Europe after the Second World War. As the situation
in Europe improved, thoughts turned to improving the lot of
those in the developing world, and today, almost sixty years on,
Christian Aid is at work in over sixty countries worldwide. Its
basic motto is 'To strengthen the poor', and this it does primarily
by working through local agencies on the basis that those on the
ground know best what is needed and what will work. In recent
years there has been a need for Christian Aid personnel to be
present locally in some areas in order that there may be greater
accountability, but the principle of working through local agencies remains paramount. The organisation is owned by over
forty churches and religious communities on these islands, and
it was my privilege to serve on the Central Board for eight years.
Canon Desmond Harman had served on the Board previously
and Bishop Michael Mayes is currently a member.

Looking back to the Advisory Committee set up prior to the
inauguration of the Bishops' Appeal, it's of interest to note that
they were charged with submitting a plan to the Standing
Committee which would enable the Church of Ireland to formu-
late a budgetary policy to 'encourage each member to become
involved in Christian Aid and World Development'.

For me becoming involved in Christian Aid has taken a variety of forms: support of Christian Aid Week events; responding
to emergency appeals; ensuring that funds from the Bishops'
Appeal were channelled to appropriate Christian Aid projects;
as a member of the Christian Aid Board endeavouring to keep
the bishops and the Church of Ireland at large in touch with ongoing developments and thinking at central level. However,
shortly before I retired in 1998 I was invited to be part of a

Christian Aid delegation to the Dominican Republic which more than any other experience was to leave a lasting impression.

The traveller arriving at Santo Domingo airport in the Dominican Republic is greeting by an exotic poster: 'Welcome to the Paradise of Paradises.' On the face of it there is some truth in the claim, with the blue Caribbean Sea, swaying palm trees and brilliant sunshine creating a setting which has led to the Dominican Republic becoming one of the fastest growing holiday destinations in the world. However, scratch below the surface and the picture changes to one of abject poverty, and at that time a denial of human rights to a large section of the inhabitants i.e. the Haitian population and the Dominicans of Haitian origin within the country.

The Dominican Republic forms two thirds of the island of Hispaniola in the Caribbean, the other third forming Haiti, one of the poorest countries in the world. The Dominican Republic was colonised by Spain in the early sixteenth century, but it was never a significant economic colony until cattle ranching was established which required less slave labour than the more intensive sugar plantations of Haiti which was colonised by the French. This meant that fewer African slaves were incorporated into Dominican society. In 1804 the slaves of Haiti revolted against their colonial regime and the country was proclaimed the 'first black republic in the Western hemisphere'. Following independence, Haiti invaded its Spanish neighbour in an attempt to unite the island. This finally occurred in 1822, but in 1844 the Dominican Republic gained its independence, not from Spain but from Haiti.

This period of history has left a sour taste in the mouth of many Dominicans. Black people are perceived as a threat, and in referring to themselves Dominicans speak of being chocolate in colour rather than black.

Because of the economic situation in Haiti, thousands of Haitians cross the border to seek work in the Dominican Republic. Many become illegal immigrants, of which there are reckoned to be between 600,000 and 800,000. Because they lack legal documents these people are under constant threat of deportation and this happens to many thousands each year despite the fact that they contribute substantially to the economy of the country by doing tasks which Dominicans are reluctant for perform. This is particularly true of those who work on the sugar plantations and live in sub-human conditions in what are called *bateyes* or specially constructed villages either close to a sugar mill or in the middle of a cane plantation.

It was in an attempt to gain in understanding of this situation and to show solidarity with the marginalised and with those organisations seeking social change that the Christian Aid delegation set out for the Dominican Republic. The six members of the delegation represented a wide spectrum of church life and backgrounds, and during the ten day visit met a variety of people including Dominican government ministers, the Haitian Chargé d'Affairs, a number of NGOs and church leaders, and most important of all visited and talked with those Haitians who were at the centre of our concern.

It was of interest that the delegation was viewed by the Dominican Department of Foreign Affairs as complementing two previous delegations from the UN and the USA.

On returning home, members of the delegation in their various contexts attempted to alert those in positions of political influence to the plight of the Haitian immigrant population, but one had the suspicion that there were more pressing matters on their agendas. In one radio interview I was asked if I thought that our visit had really served any useful purpose. I suggested that the visit should not be viewed in isolation but part of an overall attempt to bring pressure to bear on the Dominican government, and in any case sometimes it is a matter of casting bread upon the waters in the hope that it will return enhanced. That hope was in fact realised when in the Autumn 2000 edition of *Christian Aid News* there appeared the headline: 'Victory for Human Rights in the Dominican Republic,' and below it the following account:

A Christian Aid partner has won a major legal battle against the Government of the Dominican Republic over the mass deportation of Dominico-Haitian and Haitian migrant workers. MUDHA (Movement of Dominico-Haitian Woman) also raised individual cases of several Dominican citizens who had been illegally deported because of their ethnic background. Sonia Pierre, co-ordinator of MUDHA, and Padre Pedro Ruquoy, a Catholic priest, brought the case to the Inter-American Court on Human Rights in May following the repatriation of approximately 20,000 Dominico-Haitians and Haitians by the Dominican Government last year. In August the court ruled that the individuals concerned should be allowed to return to the Dominican Republic and ordered the Government to submit regular reports both on the condition of the bateyes and on the deportations. It also ruled that the Government must alter its highly contentious migration policy proposals.

Such is some of the hard graft and unspectacular work supported by Christian Aid, in addition to the more headline grabbing activity in times of crisis. Because of its historic association with Christian Aid the Church of Ireland, through the Bishops' Appeal, can feel a genuine part of this ongoing work, which has at its root the goal of strengthening the poor.

CHAPTER 11

The Changing Scenes of Life

Throughout Ireland there are a variety of institutions associated with particular dioceses, most often to do with education, medicine or housing. St Luke's Home in Cork is one such establishment. Founded in 1872 by Frances (Fanny) Gregg, daughter of John Gregg, Bishop of Cork, Cloyne and Ross from 1862 to 1878, the original Home was on Victoria Road and catered for eighteen patients, or residents as they are now referred to. As the original name, Home for Protestant Incurables (HPI), would indicate, it had a specific clientele in mind, which really reflected the tenor of the age. In 1879 a new and larger Home catering for over one hundred residents was opened on Military Road and dedicated by the Rt Rev Robert Samuel Gregg, Fanny's brother, who had succeeded his father as bishop. The new home continued to reflect the religious ethos of the times. In its structure and layout it also reflected the contemporary approach to the sick, who were catered for in large dormitory type wards with little or no sense of privacy. Despite this there was a distinctive atmosphere of care associated with the Home which owed much to the dedication of the staff.

Such was the situation when I arrived in 1988 to take up the inherited role of Chairman of the Council, and for a few short years that task was comparatively tranquil as we met in the Boardroom each month, alert to the eagle eye of Miss Peg Exham who ensured that we all paid our £2 for lunch. However, a number of circumstances combined to disturb the calm waters of tranquillity and turn the Council's mind to changing circumstances: the cost of implementing the Nursing Homes' Act; new fire regulations estimated to cost one million pounds; recurring deficits that were forecast to lead to closure within five years; a changing attitude to the care of the elderly which was inhibited by the layout of the current Home. Added to these factors was a reappraisal of the relevance of the Memorandum and Articles of Association to contemporary society.

Gradually the Council came to realise that the only way the problems could be met was by a move to a green-field site and a redrafting of the Memorandum and Articles by which the Home could become inclusive rather than exclusive. Brave and visionary decisions were taken, the Memorandum and Articles were adopted, and a site was acquired at Mahon as a prelude to the opening of the new Home in 1994.

Through all the changing scenes those involved were greatly encouraged by the Lords Mayor, initially by Micheál Martin, now Minister for Health, and also by John Murray in the crucial year of 1993. Indeed, but for the good offices of the latter, the Council might not have been in a position to move forward. The story of his direct involvement is worth recounting. It was estimated that the cost of building would be four million pounds, but one million pounds was needed to kick-start the project. It was hoped that this would be forthcoming from the Department of Health. John Murray arranged for a delegation from St Luke's to meet the Minister, Brendan Howlin, in Dublin. On the appointed day, Gordon Baker (Chairman of the Design Team), Michael Lyons (Administrator), John Murray and myself travelled to Dublin in the mayoral car. As a result of the meeting the million pounds was assured, enabling Council to make the historic decision to move. So began a period of intense activity, culminating in December 1994 in the movement of the residents to the new Home. St Luke's is recognised as a flagship of its type, and is regularly visited by those involved in the care of the elderly.

It was inevitable that with such far-reaching changes there would be misgivings on the part of some who sought sanctuary in the *status quo*. However, change was inevitable, and the Council was is no doubt that it was better to initiate it and have some say in the matter than to be overtaken by it. The history of St Luke's since its beginning can be found in Annie Stephen's book *Luke Here* produced in 1997 to celebrate the 125th anniversary of the Home.

CHAPTER 12

Focus on Unity

By tradition there are a number of tasks associated with a bishop – president at the eucharist, guardian of the faith, encourager of mission, representative figure both to the church at large and to the community, and *pastor pastorum*. In addition there are the two tasks specifically identified with the bishop, ordination and confirmation, possibly the two most satisfying duties associated with the episcopal office. Because people's gifts, abilities and predilections vary, the emphasis in the exercise of *episcopé* varies also, and care must be taken that the balance does not become too heavily tilted in one direction to the detriment of others. Ecclesiastically speaking we all have different centres of gravity, not to mention the baggage already referred to.

However, there is one role which in recent years has come to the fore and that is the bishop as a focus of unity.

We usually think of this in terms of ecumenism, but in fact it is a multifaceted role involving the diocesan family, the ecumenical scene and the wider Anglican Communion.

Let me begin by taking this last aspect first and basing my comments on experiences at the Lambeth Conferences of 1988 and 1998.

1988 was the first occasion when members of the Anglican Consultative Council were present at Lambeth. The chairman of the ACC at that time was the then Archdeacon of Sabah in South East Asia, Datuk Ping Chung Yong. As is often the case with people from the Far East he had a boyish look which not even his work as archdeacon had managed to dispel! He appeared to be something of a lonely figure at Lambeth '88, not being quite sure what his role was there, but as chair of the ACC he was a man of proven ability with, one assumes, a strong feel for the place of Anglicanism in the worldwide Christian family of churches. Because we were in the same residence, my wife and I came to know him quite well, and were interested to learn a few years later of his appointment as Bishop of Sabah.

Come Lambeth 1998 and I found myself in the same small working group as Yong Ping Chung. As the three weeks of the conference progressed, I and the other members of the group came to know him at a deeper level through our mutual sharing of thoughts and experiences.

On one particular occasion as we shared our experiences of working under stress, Yong Ping Chung told of the problems he sometimes had to face from Western missionaries, who came with readymade solutions to problems they didn't understand because, as he maintained, they didn't understand the Eastern mind. I can still picture him speaking with great intensity, and culminating with the plea, 'Leave us to solve our own problems.'

Within a year or so he succeeded Moses Tay as Archbishop of South East Asia, and shortly after that he participated in the irregular consecration of three priests from the Episcopal Church of the United States of America (ECUSA). I have found this to be one of the most disquieting episodes of the post Lambeth period. Not only was it an about turn at the personal level on the part of someone whose *modus operandi* was summed up by 'leave us to solve our own problems', but it struck at the very heart of that unity which episcopacy represents and is intended to safeguard, and is explored in depth in the Virginia Report which was part of the Lambeth '98 preparatory material. Certainly the ordinal of the Church of Ireland is very clear on this matter: 'Will you promote unity, peace and love among all Christian people, and especially among those whom you serve?'

It is this latter phrase, 'especially among those whom you serve', that indicates the other two domains where a bishop acts as a focus of unity. On the one hand there is the wider Christian community, and on the other hand the diocesan family.

First the wider Christian community:

In approaching this issue one does so with diffidence conscious that in some dioceses even to mention the world 'ecumenism' is to court hostility. Nevertheless it must be faced if we are to come to terms with Our Lord's high priestly prayer, 'that they all may be one'. Not to do so is to fall into the trap of biblical selectivity. It was Hans Küng who said, 'to be a Christian is to be an ecumenical Christian', a thought further stressed, for example, in the Rule of Taizé which states: 'Never resign yourself to the scandal of the separation of Christians. Be consumed with burning zeal for the unity of the Body of Christ.'

During my sojourn in Cork I enjoyed very happy relations with the leaders of the other major Christian traditions: Alan Haughton (Society of Friends), Robin Roddie and Kenneth Todd (Methodist), Brian Graeme Cook and John Faris (Presbyterian) and Michael Murphy and John Buckley (Roman Catholic), while the first letter of welcome I received on my appointment to the United Diocese was from the Bishop of Cloyne, Dr John Magee.

Those with reasonably long memories will understand that relationships at the episcopal level in Cork were not always as cordial, and there was a time when the confirmation addresses of Bishop Lucey were notorious as vehicles of triumphalism. Those days were far removed from the joint staff meetings I enjoyed with Bishop Murphy, and the happy working relationship I had with his assistant, now diocesan bishop, John Buckley. I reckon that my time in Cork was a period of bridge building based on the foundation laid by my predecessor, Dr Samuel Poyntz.

This good relationship could be re-echoed throughout the country from diocese to diocese, despite the plethora of documents that have emerged from the Roman Catholic Church in recent times, including the *Directory for the Application of Principles and Norms on Ecumenism* in 1993. This is a mixture of ecumenical idealism and thinly veiled triumphal assertion, which makes it more difficult to sustain the ecumenical vision at the episcopal level.

It is at such times that one clings to whatever lifelines are available. One such lifeline is contained in the report of the 10th Assembly of the Conference of European Churches (CEC) which stated, 'Unity is not an end of diversity, but of division,' a though re-echoed some years ago (1977) by Bishop John Bothwell of Niagara on the occasion of the ordination of the first women priests in Canada: 'Witnessing to our diversity without breaking the bonds of love.' Unity and diversity are the twin concepts which must be kept in balance as a bishop seeks to be true to his/her consecration promise.

Often that promise is most specifically tested as a bishop seeks to respond to it within his own diocese: 'Will you promote unity, peace and love ... especially among those whom you serve?'

If one thinks of a diocese in terms of a human family it is inevitable that there will be differences, tensions, problems. To imagine otherwise is to live in cloud cuckoo land. Here in the context of the diocese the concept of unity in diversity is often most sorely tested. Here the role of the bishop as a focus of unity is most clearly identified but at times most seriously challenged. It's a role which has become increasingly difficult to exercise as the church has come to be dominated more and more by issues which tend to polarise people into camps. We have seen this in relation to such matters as church closures and Drumcree, but there is one other issue which must be mentioned because both at parochial and diocesan level it has stalked the Church of Ireland for the past forty years, and that is liturgical revision.

It was inevitable that the Church of Ireland would be caught up in the surge of worldwide liturgical revision from the 1960s onwards, and the setting up of the Liturgical Advisory Committee in 1962 reflected this. But my mind goes back specifically to Armagh Cathedral in 1984 and the service introducing the *Alternative Prayer Book,* which marked the climax of the primacy of Archbishop John Armstrong. The preacher was to be the Archbishop of Wales, Derrick Childs, but bad weather precluded him from being present and his sermon was read by John Armstrong.

Like the majority of sermons I have forgotten most of what it contained, but one point has stuck in my mind to this day. Archbishop Childs questioned the wisdom of having two prayer books, because he said it would encourage division. Perhaps it was the only way forward in the Church of Ireland at the time if a revised liturgy was to be accepted by General Synod, but divisive it certainly has been, as many a rector can testify. In some dioceses, rather like the introduction of the Euro, the issue was addressed by an episcopal dictat, and while a semblance of unity was no doubt achieved, a question mark must be placed over the long-term effect on relationships in certain parishes. It may well be that the prayer book to be introduced in 2004 will

restore a sense of liturgical unity, and the divisive trend envis-
aged by Archbishop Childs in 1984 will be reversed. It surely is
ironic that what at one time was a cord binding people together
and acting as an instrument of unity, common prayer, should
have become a divisive issue in the church, consequently making the role of the bishop as focus of unity more difficult to exercise. Couple this with a DIY mentality characteristic of some
clergy, and the cord of unity, which should be a feature of
Anglican worship, becomes even more tenuous. But as might be
commented on in certain quarters, *sin scéal eile.*

At the heart of Anglican worship is the Eucharist or Holy
Communion, and in recent years there has been an open invitation to all those who receive communion in their own churches.
While this has never been formalised by legislation in the
Church of Ireland, its development can be traced back to
Lambeth 1968 where Resolutions 45, 46 and 47 deal with the
subject. As already stated Lambeth resolutions do not have legislative authority in individual provinces, but they do carry the
moral weight of consensus, and for that reason are important to
recall as the churches seek to express their unity 'that the world
may believe', or at least take their talk of unity seriously.

Admission of Non-Anglicans to Holy Communion
45. The Conference recommends that, in order to meet special pastoral needs of God's people, under the direction of the
bishop Christians duly baptised in the name of the Holy
Trinity and qualified to receive Holy Communion in their
own churches may be welcomed at the Lord's table in the
Anglican Communion.

Anglicans Communicating in other than Anglican Churches
46. The Conference recommends that, while it is the general
practice of the church that Anglican communicants receive the
Holy Communion at the hands of ordained ministers of their
own church or of churches in communion therewith, nevertheless under the general direction of the bishop, to meet special pastoral need, such communicants be free to attend the
Eucharist in other churches holding the apostolic faith as contained in the scriptures and summarised in the Apostles' and
Nicene Creeds, and as conscience dictates to receive the sacra-
ment, when they know they are welcome to do so.

Reciprocal Acts of Intercommunion.

47. The Conference recommends that, where there is agreement between an Anglican Church and some other church or churches to seek unity in a way which includes agreement on apostolic faith and order, and where that agreement to seek unity has found expression, whether in a covenant to unite or in some other appropriate form, a church of the Anglican Communion should be free to allow reciprocal acts of inter-communion under the general direction of the bishop; each province concerned to determine when the negotiations for union in which it is engaged have reached the stage which allows this inter-communion.

Generally speaking there are two attitudes to sharing the eucharist. On the one hand there are those who see it as a means to an end, an instrument in achieving visible, organic unity. On the other hand, are those who see it as the goal of unity and the ultimate expression of ecumenism. It is an issue that surfaces from time to time, usually in well publicised circumstances. At such times my thoughts go back over forty years to a World Student Christian Federation Conference (WSCF) in America in 1960. The main speaker was Bishop Leslie Newbiggen of the Church of South India. The final act of worship was to be a Holy Communion service, and on the evening before Bishop Newbiggen addressed the great gathering of four thousand students. He spoke of the service on the following day and asked those who intended going to grapple with what it would mean to them. He suggested that those going were making a commitment to serve the ecumenical movement. It was not be viewed as a one off event to be taken in isolation, nor to be regarded as a defiant gesture towards their own church's discipline, whatever that might be. They were wise words and no less relevant today than they were forty years ago.

At a strictly non-ecclesial level much is done throughout the country that brings people together in humanitarian causes. This was highlighted in Cork by the Chernobyl Project, spearheaded by Adi Roche, whose powers of motivation are truly remarkable. Each year Irish homes open their doors to children from Belarus and convoys of trucks leave regularly on the hazardous journey across Europe. This and similar humanitarian

projects have an ecumenical dimension that must not be dis-
counted. As people work together a bond is formed without
which theological conformity can be a very barren concept.

In Cork for many years there has been a Jewish community,
albeit a diminishing one in recent times. One who served as
Lord Mayor before my arrival was Gerald Goldberg, a man of
immense strength and character. During the 1990s the Jewish
community was ably represented by Fred Rosehill, and the
happy interfaith relations were to be seen in his willingness to
explain the significance of the Passover to Sunday Schools
throughout the diocese.

CHAPTER 13

The Three Rs

Looking back over the years as a parochial clergyman, few if any areas of work took up more time than education in its many facets. I soon discovered on being appointed as Bishop of Cork that education would continue to be a high priority in my timetable. There were three levels of involvement: primary, secondary and tertiary.

At the primary level the bishop is patron of the schools in the diocese, and it is this patronage that defines the schools as Church of Ireland. Every four years he appoints representatives to the Boards of Management and nominates the chairmen. He is assisted in this work by the Diocesan Board of Education which he chairs, and indeed without the accumulated wisdom of the Board the work of the patron would be much more difficult. Usually matters run smoothly, and the debt of gratitude owed to those who serve on Boards of Management is incalculable. This is especially true of the chairmen, who at any given time may find themselves involved in protracted negotiations with the Department of Education, conflict resolution *vis-à-vis* staff members or placating irate parents, to mention but some of the circumstances that may have to be addressed.

When Boards of Management were initiated a deliberate policy of having lay chairmen was pursued in Cork diocese. It is a policy which by and large has worked well and could with profit be followed by other dioceses. The one major component that must be present is a good working relationship not just between chairman and principal, which goes without saying, but also between chairman and rector. Even though he may not be chairman, the rector has a vital pastoral responsibility towards the staff and pupils in the school.

It is one of the privileges of a bishop to visit the schools of which he is patron. In retrospect this task provided me with some of my happiest memories of Cork. The welcome by staff was never less than warm-hearted and sincere, while my visits to the classrooms invariably threw up a variety of searching questions, insightful comments and amusing incidents, often from the youngest pupils. I was invariably challenged as to my motivation in becoming a bishop and, before that, in entering the ministry.

One particular incident is worth recounting as I'm reliably informed it has entered the realms of diocesan folklore! I had arranged to visit a particular school. On the appointed day I arrived and after assembly went to each classroom in turn. I was greeted in each by the well-tutored pupils, 'Good morning, bishop.' When I came to meet third and fourth classes I suggested that the bishop had a name, and did anybody know my name. There was a loud silence, so to speak. I repeated the question, and again silence. Then a little lad at the back of the class raised his hand, and one could feel the sense of relief, especially on the part of the teacher! 'Well,' I asked, 'what is my name?' And the reply came back in a delightful Cork accent, 'Casey' – out of the mouths …!

In relation to the primary schools in Cork it's of interest that Máire Roycroft, principal of St Luke's School, Douglas, holds the distinction of being the longest serving primary school principal in Cork city. She was an invaluable resource person, and her advice was invariably tempered with her own particular brand of humour. She was a product of that nursery of primary teachers, West Cork.

Episcopal involvement at secondary level in Cork is no less onerous with three schools categorised as Protestant, at least in the eyes of the Department of Education: Midleton College, Bandon Grammar School and Ashton.

Midleton and Bandon are long established educational institutions and the bishop customarily serves on the two Boards. In both cases it was an enriching experience to be part of dedicated teams of laity and clergy whose sole objective was to serve the best interests of the schools involved. In a real sense they typified all that was best in a long-standing tradition of unselfish service. For the record the chairman of the two Boards were Professor Trevor West (Midleton) whose father had been headmaster from 1928 to 1960, and Canon J. L. B. Deane (Bandon), one of the first laymen to be honoured by being made a Canon of Armagh Cathedral by the Primate, Archbishop Eames.

In addition to serving on the Board, the bishop has the privilege of presiding at occasional services for the pupils, and of meeting them for what politicians might describe as full and frank discussion.

Ashton came under a different heading as a Protestant Comprehensive School, set up in 1973 by the amalgamation of Rochelle School and Cork Grammar School. It is one of five such schools in the Republic designed to cater specifically for the Protestant community in the wake of the introduction of free education by the late and then Minister of Education, Donogh O'Malley. Its Board consisted of five members: a representative of the Department of Education, a representative of the local Vocational Education Committee, two nominees of the bishop, with the bishop or his nominee as chairman. The school principal acted as secretary.

We were singularly fortunate in the membership of the Ashton Board. Continuing previous practice I acted as chairman, and was fortunate that the Principal, Victor Bond, was one of the few people I knew prior to coming to Cork. In addition his reputation as an educationalist was high among his peers. He retired in 1996 and was succeeded by Charles Payne, the Vice-Principal, under whose guidance the school continued to flourish.

During my time as Chairman of the Board a number of developments took place which in a sense demonstrated the changing atmosphere of education in the Cork area. From the outset Rochelle House had been retained as a boarding establishment for Ashton. When I arrived in 1988 there were over ninety boarders. By the time I left in 1998 that number was reduced to just over twenty, and one of my last duties was to preside over the Rochelle House committee when the decision to close was taken. There was an inevitability about the decision which reflected the general trend with regard to boarding throughout the country.

Although a Protestant Comprehensive School, this did not preclude entry to those of other religions traditions or none once

places were available. In 1988 there were comparatively few
such places, but ten years later about 50% of the pupils were
non-Protestant. To some extent this indicated a fall in the local
Protestant population. But there was another factor which was
affecting not only Ashton, but Bandon and Midleton also. More
and more people were sending their children to local community
colleges and schools. This was particularly so with regard to
Schull Community College, where at one stage there were upwards of thirty Protestant pupils attending. In the mid-90s when
a diocesan retreat for such pupils was organised by the Youth
Chaplain, the Rev Janet Catterall, one hundred and ten young
people attended the event. I invariably found that relationships
between the local rector and the school principal were excellent,
and for some parents, apart from the financial aspect, it was a
means of identifying with the community. There was often a
fear that once children went away to board they would not return in the long term, with consequent problems for the farming
community in terms of manpower and inheritance, not to mention a loss of input to the locality in general.

Having come from serving on a Dublin school board which
numbered thirty six, it was an interesting experience to preside
over one of five members. By judicious appointments one ensured that parents were always represented. However throughout the 1990s there was growing pressure to have both staff and
parents represented in their own right, and I am sure it is only a
matter of time before this development takes place. When it
does it will be important for those chosen to recognise that they
are members of a Board and not merely representing sectional
interests. It is not always easy to divorce oneself from the elec-
torate and concentrate on the larger picture.

Prior to going to Cork I had no experience of administration
at the tertiary level. On taking up duty I found myself on the
Governing Body of University College Cork, as by tradition the
Minister for Education, who had three nominees, appointed the
two bishops and the President of the Students' Union. It was an
invigorating experience and one I valued greatly, even though
at times it was traumatic as one came to appreciate that academic
infighting can be cut-throat in the extreme. Fortunately there
were some outstanding reconcilers on the Governing Body, men

such as Pádraig Ó Ríordáin, Principal of Douglas Community School, and Archbishop Dermot Clifford of Cashel.

However my tenure of office came to an end in 1998 with the appointment of a new Governing Body having regard to the provisions of the Universities Act 1997. For some time it had been mooted that more people with entrepreneurial skills were needed to meet the financial challenges of the future, especially in relation to research grants. As a result the then Minister for Education, Micheál Martin, TD for Cork South Central, appointed three local constituents to the Governing Body in place of the two bishops and the Student Union President. I have no doubt that this brought added expertise to the boardroom but it was received with mixed feelings if correspondence and phone calls were anything to go by. I always felt that the presence of the Church of Ireland bishop on the Governing Body set down a marker for a minority section of the community, and it was one way of giving tangible expression to the undoubted ecumenical ethos of the university and the pluralism inherent in both its staff and student body.

At a personal level I have always felt saddened that it was not until five months later at the end of May I received a communication from the Minister. It was followed up in July by an invitation to join the Board of An Gaisce, The President's Award. I accepted the invitation, and spent three fascinating years as part of an organisation which is held in the highest regard internationally, and at home encourages young people to develop their talents in a non-competitive atmosphere. It currently owes much to the genuine interest displayed by President Mc Aleese herself. Her patronage is far from being merely formal.

Association with the University was not limited to administration, and it was a privilege to be present at functions with such distinguished speakers as Peter Sutherland, Mo Mowlam and Wim Duisenberg.

Occasionally I was invited to participate in a debate by one of the College Societies, and on one such occasion my failure to double check the facts caused personal embarrassment and general hilarity. The subject for debate was the advisability of having a sex shop in Cork. One had just been opened, and I was asked to contribute to the debate. By way of preparation I checked with a local cleric how a similar shop in Limerick was doing. 'Oh! It has gone out of business' was his rely. Armed with this information I made my speech and suggested that time would tell if the venture in Cork would succeed. I was immediately ridiculed by the proprietor of the Cork shop who said that the Limerick shop was not only open but flourishing, and this only went to show once again how the church was out of touch with reality!

Any reference to the university would be incomplete without paying tribute to the work of successive Church of Ireland chaplains: Maurice Carey, Richard Clarke and Michael Jackson. As Deans of Cork and rectors of the Cathedral parish they had hectic schedules, yet their ministry to all sections of the university was invaluable, and St Fin Barre's Cathedral was a place where more and more members of the College body were finding a spiritual home.

CHAPTER 14

For whom the bell tolls

31 December 1998 was a cold winter's evening as my wife and I set out from Cork to travel the twenty miles to Bandon, where we had been invited to spend New Year's Eve with the rector and his family. It was a thoughtful and appropriate gesture on this my last few hours in the active ministry and also as bishop of the diocese. Ten years earlier in St Fin Barre's Cathedral Michael Burrows was the first priest I had the privilege of ordaining, and his father, Canon Walter Burrows, had conducted the pre-ordination retreat for our class of ordinands in 1953. In a dual sense there had been a full turn of the wheel.

There was at that time a goodly and Godly tradition in Bandon that the rector and parishioners meet at the entrance to St Peter's church on New Year's Eve to bid adieu to the old year and welcome in the new one. Nothing elaborate, just a quiet waiting in the presence of God for the bell to signify the omega and the alpha. I was very conscious that on this occasion the bell was tolling for me, and also for my wife. We would return to Cork later that evening divested of the rights and privileges of office, and also no longer responsible for the well being of the diocese and its clergy. One could not help but contrast the setting on that New Year's Eve with the splendour and dignity of the consecration ceremony almost eleven years before, and the three packed and very moving enthronement services in the cathedrals of the diocese. True there were much-valued liturgical and social farewells, but at the actual moment of 'departure' one felt that there was an indefinable void.

Within the Church of Ireland very little is done to prepare the person elected or appointed bishop for the work that lies ahead. It is as though one is expected to don the mantle of episcopacy and assume almost infallible powers overnight. A short retreat

83

and in at the deep end. Despite the emphasis laid on preparation at successive Lambeth Conferences there is still a long way to go when contrasted with other parts of the Anglican Communion. One felt positively envious of the first lady diocesan bishop in New Zealand, Penny Jamieson, who spent a month in Scotland by way of preparation.

As it was at the beginning so it was at the end. Apart from the constitutional requirement to inform the archbishop of the province of one's intention to retire on a specific date there is no other obligation to prepare for retirement. Friends in other professions express surprise at this, and in more and more branches of life preparation for retirement is assuming greater importance. This is understandable with many more people opting for early retirement.

Within the Church of Ireland earlier retirement is also a factor in the modern equation. No longer are clergy forced to remain in office and in many cases die in harness.

Pensions arrangements are such that the words of the former Bishop of Kilmore, Dr Moore, at the General Synod in 1975, when clergy were linked into the State system, reflect the situation for most clergy: 'It will enable retired clergy to live in reasonable comfort.' As a result of the more realistic pension provisions the mid-sixties are now becoming the norm for retirement. While this creates inevitable problems in staffing parishes, it does mean that a large number of parochial clergy and bishops can look forward to some years of active retirement. Indeed it's of interest to reflect that the number of retired bishops now equals the number of those in the House of Bishops. This may well be the first time that such a situation has arisen.

No doubt many are well capable of preparing for retirement in a positive way, but there is surely a case to be made for some form of preparation for this newfound freedom from responsibility.

In recent years much emphasis has been laid on clerical stress, focusing largely on the nature of the work, not least the number of hours involved and the isolation of many clergy, particularly in rural areas. Could it be that there is also an underlying worry about the future? As one senior cleric responded when asked about retirement – 'But what would I do?'

There is also the decision to be made where one retires. To retire within the parish or diocese means that one does not have to move out from the familiar locality, especially if the tenure of office has been lengthy. On the other hand it can pose obvious problems for one's successor, and the Church of Ireland is littered with parishes where the tensions of residential retirement are obvious.

Coupled with the retirement of the cleric is the 'retirement' of his/her spouse. One suspects that this relates more to the clergy wife than the clergy husband. Although having said that, one is conscious that more and more pursue their own careers than in years gone by, and there are certainly husbands who devote themselves to full-time support.

Views differ on the role of the spouse. Obviously it must be supportive; otherwise tensions will arise within the home. This is most demanding for late ordinands and their spouses who may have been accustomed to a particular lifestyle in their former profession.

But support must not spill over into aping the role of a cleric. The two members of 'the team', as it is sometimes referred to, must recognise that only one is ordained, and ordination brings with it obligations of confidentiality. Nothing is more calculated to undermine the trust of parishioners than the feeling that matters spoken of in confidence are being discussed in the Rectory or See House. Probably the most valuable piece of advice given to my wife by her rector before we were married was, 'Always remember there are some things your husband will not be able to discuss with you.' There is a certain romanticism in saying, 'There will be no secrets between us,' but in a clerical or episcopal household romanticism in that sense has certain limits.

Probably one of the most interesting forms of support was noted at the 1998 Lambeth Conference. Prior to the conference the spouses were asked to submit suggestions for a series of workshops. They ranged from mitre making to musical appreciation, but in the midst of the more mundane requests was one for a workshop on aircraft maintenance. It came from Marian McCall, wife of the Bishop of Willochra in Australia, David McCall. Because of the size of the diocese driving meant that he was absent from home for lengthy periods. His wife decided

that in order to see her husband occasionally she should learn to
fly. This would also relieve him of some of the burden of travel.
Aircraft maintenance seemed a natural follow on, and at
Lambeth her request was granted. There are indeed varied ways
of supporting one's clerical spouse, and this certainly added a
new dimension to the term 'sky pilot'.

However, the more involved a spouse is with the supportive
work of the ministry the greater the impact of retirement will be
and the greater the need for preparation. In one sense life goes
on as usual especially for a clerical wife. 'How are you enjoying
retirement' has a slightly hollow ring about it when one contem-
plates the washing machine and the dishwasher! On the other
hand it does provide an opportunity to do things together, and
this is probably the big plus. They don't have to be major projects. Fun and satisfaction are two of the main ingredients and
the opportunity to broaden one's interests and circle of friends, a
circle which of necessity is circumscribed in both the parochial
and episcopal ministry.

One of the factors that eased the trauma of retirement was
the fact that in my adopted diocese of Meath and Kildare there
were a number of former colleagues from Cork including the
bishop, archdeacon and dean, together with two rectors that I
had ordained. In addition another rector had served as curate
with me when I was rector of Zion parish in Dublin. All of which
was a reminder that diocesan boundaries are no longer the Pale-
like obstacles to movement that once they were. It was also an
illustration of the familial nature of the Church of Ireland which
is one of its most distinctive characteristics.